LET'S
GROW

JAMES
MR. SPEAKER
SEARS

Let's Grow

Copyright © 2025 James "Mr. Speaker" Sears

ISBN (Paperback): 979-8-89672-129-1
ISBN (Hardback): 979-8-89672-130-7
ISBN (Ebook): 979-8-89672-131-4

Printed in the United States of America.

PROMINENT
BOOKS
EDGE

5830 E 2nd St, Ste 7000 #9983
Casper, WY 82609
USA

DEDICATION

My mother, Catherine Patricia Sears, and I had a remarkable bond long before I even knew her name. All that I have accomplished in life is because of God and my mother.

So, on 12 July 2015 when my mother told he she was going into hospice care, I finally broke down. I had been strong throughout her two-year battle with lung and liver cancer, but she and I knew this signaled the end. My mother planned her funeral, arranged every detail, walked into hospice care like a champion. She had run an excellent race, fought a tremendous fight and she was ready to meet her maker. Two weeks off a knee replacement, I flew home to Louisville, Kentucky to read these words below that I would eventually read one month later at her home-going service.

To My Mother: Because of You!

Today, I speak over the best person I know, the foundation of my family, my confident, my advisor, my teacher, my reason, my mother.

If you knew her or knew of her, then you know she set the standard. The sun just does not shine the same the day you lose your mother. What I have dealt with are empty feelings, an aching heart, and wet eyes.

Flowers do not seem to bloom, and birds do not seem to sing, but we must Soldier on. Thank you, God, for blessing us with this life!

Because of this woman, I can cook, sew, sing, play the piano, and I hate being late for anything.

Because of her, I can sleep with the lights and TV on, I know what great food taste like, I have a green thumb, I've sang in many choirs, I'm a fighter and not a quitter, I know how to skate, I can drive, I love being around family, I'm a morning person, and I know how to plan, especially family reunions.

Because of Catherine Sears, I know the Bible and I know every parable in the Bible, and I have scriptures written on my heart.

You had to recite Bible verses in her home and in her car! Because of her, we were the first family at Church every Sunday, Sunday school was mandatory because she was a Sunday School teacher, and I mopped the Church's flooded basement floor at the old building more times than I can remember. I grew up in Burnett Avenue Baptist Church.

Because of her, I am a graduate of Louisville Male High School, I am a Soldier and not a Sailor, and I have a heart for helping people. Because of her, I am the first college graduate in my family, I am a teacher, coach, and mentor. I have traveled the world, I have created leadership environments that allow Soldiers to thrive, and I have achieved greatness within the United States military.

Because of my mother, I have published two books, three CDs, own several homes and cars, I know how to pray, and I have a master's degree. Because of her, General Electric is me!

I am telling you this because, a teacher once told my mother that she would not amount to much at all. That is why my mother was not shy at all to say, "But look at my son."

I had a front row seat to witness this woman bless generations of her family, my Church, and many she contacted.

Back in the day, when this woman got her first car, she drove from the east end of Louisville to the west end, stuffed 10 or more kids in her car and brought them to Burnett Avenue every Sunday morning for Sunday School.

Because of this woman, Burnett Avenues Baptist Church has Johnsons, Slemmons, Coleys, Lathams, Coopers, Bennetts, Cunninghams, and the Sears families, just to name a few.

She has so many family members in this Church, that she was lovingly called a DON! She loved her family, and she loved her Church. My mother actually called a family meeting and told everyone they were going to vote for Pastor Schull as our new pastor and guess who our pastor is now. This Church has been blessed beyond measure.

My mother, Catherine Patricia Sears (Mitchell) had a great run. We are all going to leave this place but are you making any differences in this world right now.

She has always been my home, my super woman, my safe space, and my mom. The best cook I will ever know.

She is the wisest and strongest person I've known with no exceptions. She once called me "Her Strength" but what she actually saw was herself in my reflection.

Rest In Peace Mom, I love you

12 July 2015

NOW, LET'S GROW!

I have been asked several times, "How do you deal with the transition of someone very close to you, particularly your mother?" Here are three things that helped me tremendously when my mother transitioned from this life.

First, I had to focus on what I received and not what I did not receive. Many times, we mourn the time we wish we had gotten with our loved ones while we are somewhat disrespecting the time we were given. Example, you had your mother in your life for 60 years and you are crying over not having them for 10 to 15 more years. Be thankful for being blessed with the 60 years you received.

Secondly, anytime I do not live up to my mother's expectation, I am disrespecting her life's work and her legacy. I was forgetting her teachings and not living up to the standards she had established. I realized, I had to live up to her expectations, maintain her standards, and honor all the guidance she provided.

Finally, I had to remember that it is a blessing for a parent to transition prior to their child. In my line of work, Soldiering, I have witnessed the heartbreak of many parents having to bury their children. When my mother transitioned before me, she was being blessed not to witness the death of her child. I thank God for Devine Order.

My hope is that you are able to consider these three things when someone close to you transitions. Be thankful for the time with them that you were blessed with, live up to what they taught you, and be thankful they did not have to bury you. Rest in Poetry!

James "Mr. Speaker" Sears

CHAPTER ONE

My Growth

CONTENTS

WHO AM I?

Hello readers, I realize some of you
may not know me, that's okay.
My moniker is Mr. Speaker, professionally
    I am called Sir. or Colonel because I'm
a modern-day Buffalo Soldier
that means on the 1st and 15th of each month I get paid; I also collect
rents. Kentucky, Virginia, and Georgia are the states from where my
money is sent.

I train Soldiers, give them orders, and guide them as we protect our
homes and residences. Check this, some of my orders come directly
from the United States President.

I shake hands with people like I am running for a
political position. I've dined with kings and played dominos with
waiters and defeated some of the best military competition.

I have traveled the world so much that right now I have three different
types of foreign currency in my pocket.
I have driven 160 miles per hour on the German Autobahn and it felt
like I was in a rocket.

Since I graduated, I have never been unemployed as I have needs that
I must feed.
Yes, I said graduated because to walk in my shoes, means you will
need at least a master's degree.
Western Kentucky and Central Michigan Universities are where I
put my university work in once I left Smoke Town.

College educated, paid, with street creditability no doubt, now that's how a true leader gets down.

Started out as an enlisted Soldier, been an artilleryman, seen Lieutenant Dan, and I have been called a Major Payne a long time ago.

Yes, I am an American guardian and life saver but to all the gold diggers, this Soldier is not your Captain Save-a-hoe.

I have been making and living some of the history you have been hearing and reading about, but the fact is, you cannot believe everything in the media and that is no doubt.

Check this, minorities commit 20% of the local crimes, that fact is crystal clear. But minority crimes get 70% of the media play which is how they keep a lot of people in fear.

Look, it is 2025 people, and the United States is trying to lead the free world once more. While it is clear some people have not even realized that the south actually lost the Civil War!

I am not afraid as I put my work in daily, have excellent credit and high clout.
Check the records and you will see I am that man
Salt N Pepper once rapped about.

Strong Kappa Man, never been incarcerated and still looking for my queen.

Being a military leader is hard work so I cannot have just anyone on my team.
Let me put it in a nutshell and give my description a little twist. So, hold on to your seats as I run it down like this.

4

LET'S GROW

I am a spiritually grounded, out-front leader and an expert logistician. Skilled motivator, extensively educated, and a gifted mathematician.

I am 100% fit-to-fight, a combat veteran, and certified expert with either hand. Deadly sniper, African heritage, leader of leaders, widely traveled, and yes, I am an All-American.

Arrogant, possibly; conceded, maybe; feared, better be respected, definitely; paid, happily; gifted, poetically; jock formally; confident, extremely; blessed both physically and spiritually!

Strapped, always; Nupe every day; hero, some say; On-target, all day; standing tall, not afraid; Run, no way!

Well, that is unless I am chasing you
then there is nothing that you can really do.

But if I am not chasing you and you see me running, well then you better catch up because there is no telling what is coming.

Bottom line, you do not want me angry and looking for you, because you will never see what is coming and I won't stop until you are through.

Run, hide, I will find you and that is no doubt and when I catch you, I will make you talk-tell all you know with torture techniques you have never heard about.

Face it, I am the closest most of you will ever get to war.
Sit down and listen when I grab the mic and take the floor.

Look, I've heard what singers like Destiny Child said and what some of those other rappers have told Ya.

But get it straight, it is me, not those street thugs who is a real live, modern-day Buffalo Soldier.

It is my job to stand strong, look danger in the eye and never quit while I can fight.

Without Soldiers like me, you can bet your freedoms would not last seven nights.

Since 1990 I have been representing the United States Army, both nationally and worldwide

That is what can happen to a man who knows the true meaning of Phi Nu Pi!

So, take a deep breath and think of me when you relax at home all safe tonight.

Because it is your home-grown, Louisville Soldier, leader of the pack, and protector of your freedoms and your Rights!

EARTH

I am an Earth poet with one foot in water spitting fire through the
air. Beware, I poet any and everywhere.

Called a didactic poet by super star Cass is Free.
Me, because I spit facts constantly and continuously, grounded,
rounded, compounded, in actuality.

The reality is I teach, in an attempt to breach gaps and reach my
peeps. You look confused so, allow me to explain Yo.

Consider me volcano, spewing facts, lava blows
cleaning pipes, Drano. Twisting words, tornado.

I bend lava flows, I'm not the Avatar though.
Called Captain save-a-ho, because I have stacks you know, lines that
flow, drop massive blows, especially while playing dominos.

I'm not finished bro. Still turning nouns into ammo.
Follow me and increase your dough.
I heard cats, leadership phenomenal.

Me, an Angel of War, spiritual and physical
I will never be po. Have you seen my four chateaus?
My everyday car rides like a limo.

Come, listen, let's grow, check my credentials, sorry, my time is low.
Hit me, I may host your show,
but for now, I'm Mr. Speaker and I have got to go

I AM LOVE

Since my mother's big, beautiful belly deflated, I was carved cut and created in His image.

Love lined and laced, literally since I leaped from my line of scrimmage.

Blessed with boldness, bouncing bravely through blockages and barricades.

No bears in caves, but liberally, lavishing, love in all languages to the lost.

And found, tone down, your verbal attack, do not sit back.

Use your fleet fortunate feet to retreat and take love, not hate to your poetic streets.

Or take love from adoration to admiration as you add more to the nation, I admire your patience.

Harken and hear with your unharden heart, no barking
Speak the light of love, lavished loosely not darken

Love binds and locks like long, luscious dread locks,
like how buildings are made of rocks, or
how your feet are hugged by socks.

Love is chocolate you can rock with, fill pockets, and sockets.

LET'S GROW

Love is air and spring, fair and refreshing.
Love is chill, spins wheels, gives thrills, breaks, builds, and hate it kills.

Love occupies your heart and melts the mind.

Love is truth, protection, honor, tough, deliberate, and kind

Come see mine then copy my agape no way you can stop me.

See, I am love, sourced from above.
Someone hate is hella sick of.

The most powerful force you can think of.
The one thing the world needs more of.

Do not blink, just wink love.
And fall into my sink love.

No need for mask or gloves.

See, hate stinks love,
from heaven to the sea.

Open your eyes, you are on the brink of me.
I am Mr. Speaker, and I am love.

I AM DEPRESSION

I am depression and I will kill every last one of you, break you down, turn smiles to frowns, just to keep you blue.

Given the chance, my goal is to devastate you, rich or sad, happy, or mad, I do not care what you want to do.

I live to destroy everything about you. My desire is to leave you bogued down, in constant rain, afraid, and confused.

Like COVID, I spread from lips to ears with a plan to silently come for you. Crushing hopes, destroying dreams, and giving you a self-hate type mode.

Respecting nothing about you, rich or poor, I do not care what you have been through. Your success, status, and goals, I will devour them like Kansas City barbecue.

My targets are first responders, veterans, republicans, democrats, Christians, atheist, and Jews. Deep inside of me, I hate the thought of every single one of you.

Muslim, gays, the weak, young, all colors, see my aim is to suffocate you,
destroy moods, and make you not even want to eat food.

Do not believe me, that's you are tuned into the wrong news. Check my stats, been killing millions annually for years, do not be confused.

Suicide is my weapon of choice and isolation is my primary method.

Come, give depression a try. I will prove to you that you cannot fly.

See, I am your own rage, turned against you!

There's no trauma bigger, for my victims, I push buttons and pull triggers.

If a mothers struggles after childbirth, you call me postpartum.

When minds are split or confused, you then call me bi-polar.

As 20 plus veterans die daily you change my name to post traumatic stress.

Do not really care what you call me,
just as long as my body count continues to rise,
while you fall,
you come, to my call,
leave a letter, say your goodbyes,
and like the pied piper, baby,
follow me to your demise.

Because the day you let depression tell you what to do,
well, that is the night poetry failed you!

I AM A PROBLEM

If you are a racist, rapist, sexist, liar, or a thief, to you
I am a problem.

If you prey on the less fortunate, or if you just like taking advantage, trust, I will be hard for you to manage. If you traffic humans or you mistreat others due to something as stupid as status or race, then it is me you will face.

Get braced, because I'm coming for your neck and head, and I won't leave a trace. Yes, I am a problem.

You may get pass some with your crap but with me, I advise you to shut your trap, or get slapped in front of your children and your spouse and pulled out your house. I am a problem.

I am educated, complicated, graduated, accomplished, credentialed, and paid. Never dumb-down and always up for physical or an intellectual fight. I will meet you and defeat you where you stand, see, I am a problem.

On the Top-Secret rolls is where I am listed, respected, honored, but do not get me twisted. When it comes to big game hunting and shooting, I am completely gifted.

I'm even more of a problem because I am protected, watched over, and guided from on-high, see it is not complicated. I'm an independent thinker and minority owned and heavenly operated.

LET'S GROW

An Angel of War who does not waiver.

Walk with confidence because I am blessed and highly favored. Baby, I am a problem.

I am expertly trained, equipped, packing, and well-studied.
Lost my mother a few years ago so now, I am cold blooded.

Excellent mathematician, former athlete, and I think like a poet continuously, so I use both sides of my brain equally.

I've faced down death and yes, I am sure I have a few mental issues. My main problem is, I do not even know how to be afraid of you.

At home in the water, on land, or in the air. I do not care, I will come for you day or night.
So, keep talking, and doing what you do while I set my sights.
Because I am coming, and I am a problem, and I won't stop until I read you your last rights!

That's James Mr. Speaker Sears, and you won't see it coming.

I AM AN APEX POET

I am an Apex Poet, not a Wal-Mart greeter. When the aliens land, it's me they want when they say, "Take us to your leader."

Top of the line, prime rib, smooth flow, five cribs, multiple whips, and I spit.
I know you are talking about me, but at least you are smart enough to not let me hear that shit.

I will bust your ass, every day of the week. They could create an eight day, and I will leap over a year and beat your ass on tomorrow's street.

Because you are weak and stupid, just ask your one friend. You are hating when you should be asking me how to make these dividends.

I drop bars, in bars, on soap boxes and in private settings or venues. You are coming for me, cool, let me just send my location directly to you.

Because I'm right here, no running, I'm a fighter; this you need to know.
I've turned into a writer but I'm always ready to throw, down.

Retired on top and still making electronic bags in my sleep.
I earn your annual pay in days, and I spent more than you are worth last week.

With little effort and even less stress.
See, truth is, it was me who got your girl that new dress.

LET'S GROW

But I did not hit it see, I just put that booty on ice.

So, play nice or she will be with me in Vegas tomorrow night.

With your broke ass, get your money up and get off that minimum wage.

Learn to spell, speak, and write and then you can get on my stage.

That's right, my stage, and my mic, that's my black 750 BMW with custom tags because it's not a loner.

See, I'm not just a member of Mr. Speaker Ink, I am the owner.

I AM A NUPE!

Fresh to death mean and clean
    Because I am a Nupe
Nothing but the truth, always working – recession proof
    Because I am a Nupe

International lover skills are world re-noun
    Called Casanova pretty boy, Don Won all over town
Always clean dressed to impress
    Highflyer, world traveler just, ask your stewardess
Bring home the bacon – Can fry it in the pan
    Ladies, we melt in your mouth – not in your hands
Cain twirling, Step master and yes, we can shoot hoops
    Who needs superman when you got the Nupes
Fat house, clean cars, cloths so slick
    Will kick a dog's butt in a minute just like Mike Vick
Check writer, always strapped while in the city
    Short or tall, Nupes are always Extra Pretty
Might be down but a Nupe is never out
    Rain or shine night or day Achievement is what we are all about.
Picture-perfect camera-ready cane stepping hands so steady. Standing
tall and looking good, too sexy for Hollywood.
January 5th, 1911 –
    Birth date of the Nupes
Astronauts, Politicians, Lawyers
    Some of them are Nupes

Chivalry is never dead
Long live those Nupes

Indiana University, Bloomington Indiana
    Birthplace of the Nupes
Many are called but few are chosen
    They all want to be the Nupes
Watch your ladies' boys
    Because here comes those Nupes
Sports legend War Hero
    Don't mess with those Nupes
Policemen, Firefighters State Troopers
    You will find some Nupes
Check the Army, Navy, Air Force and Marines
    And you will find even more Nupes
Young Girls and even Cougars Too
    They all love the Nupes
Want pretty kids,
Make love with a Nupe
GQ, SI, Time magazine check them out
    You will find some Nupes
Second Best – Not good enough
    Thank God I am a Nupe
Girls gone wild
    You better check those Nasty Nupes
Achievement is the only way
    If you want to be a Nupe
When you get into trouble
    Better find those Nupes
If your lady is missing
    You need to check those Nupes
By myself or in a group
    Because I am a Nupe
Out front leading the troops
    Because I am a Nupe
Eat Red meat – hold that soup
    Because I am a Nupe
Cold as Ice - twice as nice
    Because I am a Nupe

Pretty Boy – the Ladies Toy
Because I am a Nupe
On the scene - with Crimson & Cream
      Because I am a Nupe
All night hitting it right
      Because I am a Nupe
Debonair with savoir-faire
      Because I am a Nupe
That's right, I am a Black Night
      Because I am a Nupe
Rolls Royce - Ladies Choice
      Because I am a Nupe
Above and beyond the other groups
      Because I am a Nupe
Paid in full- that's the rule
      Because I am a Nupe
Heart taker – Money Maker
      Because I am a Nupe
Top ratings – model dating
      Because I am a Nupe
Full of fun – I never run
      Because I am a Nupe
Check Writer Freedom Fighter –
      Because I am a Nupe
Fast Lane – with my cane
      Because I am a Nupe
Hard worker – Cane Stepper
      Because I am a Nupe
Fine dining - jewelries shining
Because I am a Nupe
So, throw the YO and let them know
That's right I AM A NUPE
And when they ask you why you do what you do
Just respond Because I AM A NUPE

CHAPTER TWO

Grow in God

JUDGE LESS AND LOVE MORE

Listening to a poem is like taking a journey mentally,
and you have the right to ask, "Mr. Speaker, where are you actually taking me?"

I want to take you to a place where Palestinians and Israelis live in peace.
It is a place where good news is spread while gossip and bad news are deceased.

Let's go to a place where slower traffic actually stays to the right,
and this is a place where people walk by faith and not by sight.

This is a place where women know they are worth more than one million grams,
and it is a place where there is no road rage and there are no traffic jams.

It is a place where smiles and greetings are what we all expect,
and it is a place where men honor women and treat them with the utmost respect.

Judge less when it comes to that foreigner who may be lost or having a hard time,
love more those individuals who try to feed their families by committing crimes.

Love more that individual who is giving you poor customer service.

Today could be her first day on the job and her mistakes could be because she is very nervous.

If you are a stay-at-home-mother, you home school, or maybe you are a housewife, please do not stand in judgment of others who have to work to support their life.

Judge less someone's ignorance and pray his or her knowledge keeps expanding.
Love more through many of life's miss understandings.

Instead of trying to get even, get revenge, or settle a score,
Stop, take a deep breath, then Judge Less and find a way to Love More!

WARRIOR ANGEL

Call me Michael, archangel, God's muscle, messenger, might, heaven's bouncer, sin pouncer, evil trouncer, to God alone I answer.

Because He created me and believe this, I am good at my job as I am His strong arm.
I block evil and harm from the living and the dead.
Let it be said, never worry,
I alone know where Moses' bones are buried.

Once best buddies, bros with that slippery, singer, satan for what it is worth, I personally cast him and his team to earth, along with greed, envy, and other evils, while angels cheered and the Savior watched, knowing He would have to step in as a buffer for sin.

Some fear satan while he fears me, brought him to his knees, flung him across seas,
it was me that evicted Adam and Eve from the garden and I destroyed Sudam, and Gamoa.

See, I am God's wrath, do the math, I am undefeated at this fighting task. The Angel of war, I am! I caused evil individuals to invent the phrase, God-damn. Here he comes again, always jumps in, to protect his friends, repeatedly wins, never loses to sin.

Truth be told, I am the reason there is hell on earth. Why sin dwells in the souls of men. Why humans study the art of war and not the heart of peace.

I imprisoned those demons on your street, causing the tares to grow with the wheat. Do not dread, trust every word God said.
Conduct a search, you will see that I am the most power force on heaven or earth. This is not a game; I dominate all domains. My name, the ultimate war cry. Fighting for His glory and fame.

I am known and feared by the Christian, Jew, and those that worship Buddha and Islam.
I'm the inspiration for the Warrior's Psalm.
I am, because He is, you are, because we are.

Me, an instrument of war, God's flaming sword, the original ultimate fighter, leader of the heavenly host, commander, King of battle, never rattled, follow me if you want to live. I am the strong tower, the great wall, indestructible force, unstoppable, juggernaut, protector, no angel higher.

Gladiator, God's Communicator, call me love, as I
conquer all.
Stand with me as I stand with Him because He
will never fall.

FREE WILL

There are many differences and similarities between the
religions for the sane and the mentally ill. One of the
biggest difference is the interesting concept of free will.

The date and location of your birth were divinely decided.
You were not consulted in the selection of your family
because they were also divinely provided.

Your heart beats without your approval or you, turning an ignition,
and the sun rises and sets without your permission.

On the other hand, you should choose your friends and your
occupation. You should also choose what you wear, how
you react to things, and where you vacation.

Religion should be a choice with your heart serving as the
source. It is not true worship if the followers are serving
by force.

Mandatory religion is akin to slavery and oppression.
Free will is an open honest form of expression.

Free will claims that you are responsible for your decisions
and your direction. If you make mistakes or do the wrong
things, then there is only one person to question.

On judgement day you will have to answer for all your indiscretions.
You may as well get ready for your confession.

So, embrace the freedom of making your own choice and how great it feels. Be thankful that you have this beautiful thing called free will.

THE WORD OF TRUTH

Let's get something straight once and for all.
The savior in my Bible does not look like that white
Italian you've seen in pictures posted on walls.

Understand this, I'm not going to step to you without
doing my research. So, sit back, listen, and take notes as
I state things you may not hear in church.

The first thing we need to do in order to get to the truth
and bring insight, is to read Revelation Chapter 1 verses
14 and 15 tonight.

His head and hair were white like wool and His feet like
unto fine brass. To me, that is not enough information,
so, we need to keep moving forward on this task.

Many of the Israelites and Africans rejected the Savior
while He walked the earth. They rejected His miracles,
His teachings, and they did not believe in the virgin birth.

In order to spread Christianity to Europe, the people
needed to be swayed. The leaders created a white Savior,
with white features, and an Italian Madonna were made.

Here is a simple question you can ask your preacher,
minister, bishop, or priest. Was it difficult for the Savior and
His mother to be the only white people in the Middle East?

There were no native Caucasians born in that area or
roaming around. They were not black or white,
but it is clear
the Savior was some shade of brown.

When the Savior was born, His family fled Judaea, and
went to Egypt in order to stay alive.
There is no way that a white European family goes to Africa
to hide.

They went to Africa because they would blend in,
that should give any reasonable person a clue to the color of
His skin.

Today, the Savior's color is not as important as it was back
then. Clearly, it is more important that you believe, receive,
and repent of your sins.

You were also given other directions in 2nd Timothy
Chapter 15. You were told to "Study to shew thyself approved unto
God, a workman that needed not to be ashamed, rightly dividing the
word of truth." This is directed to you.

This is letting you know that your work is not done. There
are plenty of people not telling the total truth under the sun.

Look at all these religions, cults, and different denominations
on every hill.
The one think God did give us is "Free will."

Many just accept what is said without getting any proof.
You are responsible for determining the truth.

MODERN DAY PHARISEES

Where are today's Pharisees?
You know, those biblical scholars who tried to bring the
Savior to His knees.

Surely these individuals have not given in or given up
their roles. Are they hiding in plain sight and what are
their new goals?

Are they doing good things or are they behind
the scene conjuring evil?
Are they still trying to confuse and divide the people?

The Savior said, "These Pharisees do not do what they
preach." They study and interpret the Torah or word
but there is no love in their speech.

The Pharisee were described as a brood of vipers back
in the Savior's Day. Their lives did not match the words
they would say.

We need to study the word so we can know the truth.
We are also warned to cut off things that do not bear fruit.

We are warned against hypocrisy and other things.
We should judge less and love more if we want to see
the true King.

The modern-day Pharisee have seven woes waiting on

them when they die, and here is a rule you can live by:

If something brings you closer to the Father then be not
afraid, because it has to be of God.
Many times, we do not focus on the truth because we
are tricked into watching a fake facade.

This works the other was as well. If something takes you
away from God then it is leading you directly to hell!

Keep your head and eyes up and make sure you listen to
what is being said.
You are responsible for rightly dividing the word of truth
so, you will not be misled.

HIS HUMOR

We are made in God's image and that is not a rumor, and
There is just no doubt in my mind that God has a sense of humor.

He gave us music, dance, and words to send up praises on His behalf.
I know people without rhythm have got to make God laugh.

They try so hard to keep the rhythm, but they just have two left feet.
Try as they may, it is so funny because they cannot stay on beat.

The Word tells us to make a joyful noise unto the Lord, all ye lands,
but what about those who cannot carry a tune with both hands?

See, that is why the word noise was used in the first place.
We all laugh because we know there is only noise coming out of their
face.

People without any common sense have got to make you shake your
head and laugh too. They think they know what they are talking
about, but we all know they do not have a clue.

So, the next time you see someone off beat, hear someone out of
tune, or you witness someone with the sense of a teacup, just think,
God could be looking down and cracking himself up.

MY FAVORITE BOOK

My favorite book for what is worth,
is your basic instruction before leaving earth.

All-time best seller no other book is even close.
Controversial, complicated, but it is still read the most.

Has lasted the longest,
Provided the most guidance,
Miss used by man,
To control, deceive, and steal lands.

Full of commands, some reprimands, several demands,
Love clearly has the upper hand.

According to the Bible, human life appears to be circular.

Humans walk with God.
Humans then sin against God.
God punishes them, and humans then pray forgiveness.
God forgives and humans then walk with God until they sin again.

BLESSING PARENTS
LET'S GROW!

I was once asked what is better, a miracle or a blessing actually.
The answer is, a blessing, because a blessing can impact many
generations of your family.

Parents should bless their children generously,
in accordance, to what they can handle literally.

Parents should also speak life, wealth, and prosperity,
and reframe from passing on hatred, disparity, and bigotry.

Children will go places we may never go and see thing we
will never see.
A good man leaves an inheritance to his grandchildren,
now that is prosperity.

Stand in the gap for your children & pray for them daily.
Take your family in a new direction while breaking
generational curses biblically, purposefully, and intentionally.

Withhold no good thing from your son and raise him
to be a king. Be present for your daughters and teach
her to be a good thing.

Provoke not your children to wrath and lead them with
your heart figuratively. Being a good parent is a generational blessing
to your whole family.

CHAPTER THREE

*Let's Grow Strong
(Military)*

SPECIAL OPERATOR

Over the years many individuals have asked me
"What it is like to be a special operator."

Well, we live life in a blink, one breath and one decision
at a time. In this world we move in silence, see in
darkness, and process things at the speed of war.

We think in layers and when necessary, we bring violence and crazy
to situations.

We read between lines, see through walls, and around corners.

We hear what is not being said, because we respond to failed politics.

See, in this world, every day is a good day for a gunfight.

We walk into dangerous places and run towards things normal people
avoid.

We can smell gunpowder at a distance, jump out of
perfectly good aircraft, swim in deep dangerous waters,
sleep is strange places that is if we are ever lucky enough
to sleep at all.

We work where security clearances are as high as the Eiffel Tower.

Your "Need to know" raises my suspicions and my shooting
range is 10 times greater than Steph Curry's.

In my world, silence is communication, every meeting is a family reunion, every march a parade, every paycheck a fortune, and every meal is a feast.

My buttons, partner, do not ever push them.

Disrespect is my trigger.

Touch my family or friends and I'm pulling triggers.

We use a different form of English and good decision are forgotten.

Bad decision hunt forever while we provide safety, security, and freedom.

I am just an imperfect man, doing a very difficult job, protecting the good and bad of this flawed land.

I do not need new friends and I am only one of a tremendously long line of individuals who live, fight, defend, and die all in an effort to secure freedom and preserve peace!

BLOOD ON MY UNIFORM

Mama, mama, can you see,
  what the Army has done for me?

Stood me up and dressed me down,
  marched me all over town.

Taught me right and showed me wrong,
  ran me singing Army songs.

Hurry up and wait is what we do.
  Follow orders or you are through.

Rain or shine we never stop,
  lost all my hair at the barber shop.

Standing tall and looking good
  Ought to be in Hollywood.

Got my orders and I am out the door,
  flying to settle some political score.

The Army put me on an airplane,
  calls me by my last name.

We stand, we hold, and we fight.
  We always try to do what is right.

I washed my friend's blood out of my uniform by hand
and watched it hit the ground, then I escort the body
back to his family and hometown.

Dressed in my military best with my head up, fighting
back tears as I stepped off my flight.

I was prepared to put his remains down as I faced his
children and wife.

They asked me questions I could not answer and they
also asked me why.

Why their son, brother, friend, and husband were no
longer alive?

He earned this freedom we enjoy with his blood, sweat,
and tears. For each other we fought day and night through
pain, confusion, and fear.

He paid the ultimate price for freedom, and he gave his
youth for his military team. He was under appreciated,
poorly compensated, and inadequately resourced to an
extreme.

He was a remarkable Soldier, an honorable man, and a great friend.
He was reliable, dependable, and the best person in
the world to cover your back or rear-end.

That's what he was doing with me, see we were on a
voluntary secret mission when he lost his life.
He succeeded in protecting me while I fail him, now how
could I explain that to his wife.

He was a Soldier, a father, a leader, and he made you believe
he was fearless.

LET'S GROW

The fact is friends, good friends, sisters, and brothers
sometimes die in this type of business.
Service personnel sacrifice precious things and we have
shed many private tears.

You really do not need to know what it is like to be a Soldier.
just enjoy the freedom we secure.

We can clean uniforms, vehicles, and all the other equipment
that we are assigned.
But no one has ever actually told me how to
wash my friend's blood out of my mind.

Mama, mama can you see
What fighting wars has done to me?

Mama, mama, can you see,
That fighting wars has diminished me?

It cost us the best women and men
and if you survive the war won't end
America, America, pray for me
Only God can cure PTSD.

HONOR

Today I stood for the fallen.

This afternoon I put a reef upon his chest.
Tonight, I laid a fallen comrade to rest.

35 years 3months was his time on earth.
Wife, two small children and strangers measured his worth.

A helicopter pilot, husband, father, a life with purpose.
He joined the Army and answered the call to service.

He paid the price no family should have to pay.
His spouse now stands by his grave.

His children and wife must navigate life without this man.
Some people will just not understand.

His friends will talk about how he fought his foes.

His grand children may not hear that he was a hero.

For those who have suffered a tremendous loss, you may have heard
how the story goes.

Today I laid to rest a brother, a man, a father his children will never
ever know.

SERVICE

I get emotional when I think about my service. The people who look to me for leadership have already heard this.

I consider it a privilege to stand and defend this democracy.
I will protect this land for as long as I can breathe.
Would you stand for what you believe? Would you fight for your family's right to read? Let me teach you something you may not have picked up in history.

Contrary to popular belief, the military is not a democracy.
Freedom is not guarantee to you or me,
and the United States does not have a monopoly on commodities.
Everything that your eyes can see, could be taken away honestly. So, when I tell you I get emotional about my service to this country.

It is because I protect even those that hate me. Those that would harm my seed and show me no dignity.

That is the beauty of this country you see. We allow the tares and the wheat to grow together biblically.
One day the reaper will harvest both the tares and the wheat. That is the day when all will harvest what they have reaped.
Do what is right, the harvester is coming even if you are asleep. Make sure the reaper can identify you as being something He wants to keep, wheat!

DIMINISHED

On behalf of the President of the United States of America, we appreciate you allowing your loved one to die for freedom. I apologize that they were under resourced, partially trained, and poorly equipped. I present this flag, shaped like a heart to symbolize where we broke your family. You get a Gold Star as well, stories to tell, in order to compel others to fight for freedom.

Sometimes, many times, often times, when I tell a family their loved one is not coming home, I lie a little. Every time I lose someone in combat, I die a little.

Dear Mr. Smith, your wife gave her life for freedom, but what is heard is, bla bla bla . . . and they are never coming home. Dear Mrs. Johnson, I regret to inform you that I lost your husband in war. Dear Mrs. Jones, today, your son was lost in battle.

I do not want to discourage anyone from Service but,
when I am remined of the cost of freedom, I cry a little.

If someone does not return from a mission, I wonder why a lot.

What did I do wrong? Did I say the right things? What else could I have done?

Look at my living human remains.
War has made me a slave to the grave.

Struggling to find reasons to live. I have
nothing else to give.
From PTSD, I cannot hide.
Hmmm, just now, another veteran has died.

Weapon of choice, suicide.
This veteran is survived by pain, grief, hopelessness, and depression.

This is sad.
Makes me want to gag.

This family is broken and all I have to give them is this finely folded
flag.

Service personnel dodge bullets in war and peace.
War is an unleashed beast that loves to feast.

It is clear that war makes the mind brittle, PTSD makes you
committal, a one-way ticket to a mental hospital because every time I
lose someone, I die a little, can you even see the human remains of me?

On behalf of the President of the United States of America, the
United States Military, and a grateful nation, please accept this flag
as a symbol of our appreciation for your loved one's honorable and
faithful service.

FRACTURED - MENTAL HEALTH

Internal scars, self-constructed bars, wounds as numerous as the stars, and my words locked in jars.

Screamed out, good grief, begged for help, no relief. Who actually looks out for the chief?

Aggressive, avoidance, negative reactions, my mind tends to roam. Isolation, combat fatigue, and boiling frog syndrome.

Traveling with unshakable memories, rubbernecking my life, questioning selfies on repeat.
Sleeping with demons and crying tears that never fall to my feet.

Trauma, tragedy, terrors, (Ribbit) had all three.
Is the water in this pot getting hot to anyone besides me?

I am an Angel of War seeking peace, mistakes haunt without cease.

Frustrated, fractured, fragmented, fragile, (Ribbit) this war is in my head.
I know I can smell someone cooking frog legs.

Durability dropping dreams dashed and shattered, does a Soldier's life even matter? Limited resiliency, diminished capacity, you see half of me, then laugh at me, walk right pass me.

LET'S GROW

I have a home, but my life is in the streets.
They hide bombs in debris, trying to catch me.
Things break where my heart once beat.
Been in this boiling pot so long, cannot even be reached.

Like walking when you can't breathe,
Learning when you can't read,
or finding things when you cannot see.

Tattered, torn, tossed, no rest for a while.
You bad boss, come walk this green mile.

Now you at a loss. You want to carry this red cross, deal with this mental chaos.
You are as soft as cream sauce. Useless as used dental floss. Get lost or get Mossed.

You, nah, you, cannot be me. Living with tragedy, smiling when you're unhappy.
With two bad knees, carrying the burdens of the Army, hating your sympathy.
Poetry is my therapy. I guarantee, you do not want to see someone break by serenity.

My life, me, and tumble weeds. Your negative comments could be my IED.
Just waiting to unleash literally, to disintegrate my seed, only resting when I bleed.

It does not matter if you agree. I know PTSD is killing me.

MENTALLY WOUNDED

(Dedicated to the Service personnel fighting mental illness-Stay Strong!)

When up is to the right or when loud noises cause fright.

When squares have no lines or when poems have no punctuation or meaning. (Rhymes)
If you have pennies when you need dimes or when it is noon but feels like bedtime,
you could be mentally wounded!

Patterns follow no reason, and your thoughts commit treason.
Ice is not freeze-in, even open spaces start to squeeze you in!

You may need to seek some help because you could be the walking wounded.

Everything is off center:
You are a homeowner who lives like a renter,
when altos sound like tenors,
when it is five AM and you want to eat dinner,
or you got the victory, but you do not feel like you were ever in the game.
You could be mentally wounded.

When your mind is injured:
One plus one is a mystery,
there are words on paper, but you cannot read,
you want lemonade but keep asking for tea,
like politicians your heart and wallet do not agree,
the door is open, but you are looking for a key,
your confidence fades as nothing is a guarantee, walking into the
future but the past you cannot shake or leave.

Love is like the padding on the walls of a wounded mind.
Understanding helps keep the ink and wheels between the lines.

Compassion heals and can put you on the incline.
Kindness enables them to continue their fight and not resign,
as hundreds attempt to weather the mental storms in their wounded
minds.

ON THE FRONT LINES

On the front lines, I have seen grown men cry
I have seen young boys die.
I have seen strong wills broken.
I have seen many words go unspoken.

In foxholes, I have seen atheist call on the name of God. On the front
lines, all you have is your squad.
In the face of danger, I have seen young men act like kings. I have
also seen smart individuals do some stupid things.

On the front lines, I have seen fear stop a person cold. I have seen
life-long friendships unfold.
During combat, I have seen lives lost and lives saved.
I have seen many individuals sent to premature graves.

In war, things are repeated because every day is Ground Hog Day.
I've seen hearts broken, bonds formed, friendships made, and young
men turn gray.

I have been on the front lines so much; I do not know how to relax.
I do not know if society will welcome me back.

How can I tell what is real and what is wax.
It is so difficult to tell the different between lies and facts.

After surviving the front lines, is it even possible to get your life back?

THE GREATEST WARRIOR

Born in North Africa, Carthage, modern day Tunisia was one of the greatest military leaders ever. His name, Hannibal Barca or just Hannibal and Baraq mean thunderbolt.

Hannibal was the son of Hamilcar Barca, a statesman, who commanded the Carthaginian land forces in Sicily against the Roman military during the First Punic War. Hamilcar also led the expansion of the Carthage military in Spain. Yes, Spain, see the North African Moors conquered and held Spain for approximately 800 years. Hamilcar brought his 10-year-old son Hannibal to Spain and had him swear his hostility toward Rome.

Hannibal would go on to use some of his father's military tactics to win many great victories. Hannibal is also considered one of the greatest strategist ever, as he was famous for outflanking and surrounding the enemy with the combined forces of his infantry and cavalry.

Hannibal became commander-in-chief of the Carthaginian Army at the young age of 26. He then when on to defeat Rome in the first battle of the second Punic War. Hannibal crossed the Alps with over 50,000 infantry, 9000 cavalry, and 37 elephants to attack Rome. While crossing the Alps, he almost lost half his army, and he attacked by land because Rome controlled the Mediterranean Sea. Only 20,000 infantry, 6000 cavalry, and all the elephants survived the crossing.

Once of the other side of the Alps, Hannibal joined forces with the Gaul's (Southern France) who hated Rome. Hannibal lost vision in one eye during battle. One of Hannibal's most famous victories was the battle of Cannae. During this battle, Hannibal soundly defeated the Roman army killing almost 70,000 men while only losing 4,000 men.

Hannibal's army occupied Italy for approximately 16 years but because Rome controlled the Mediterranean, resupplies were cut off and the Roman army was able to study Hannibal's tactics and reconstitute. The Roman generals then attached Carthage which devastated Hannibal's army. Hannibal returned to North Africa and was defeated by Roman military

Hannibal attacked Rome a few more times, lost, was exiled, and finally took his own life by ingesting a vial of poison because he refused to be made a prisoner of Rome. Once all the smoke cleared, Hannibal was considered one of the greatest military generals of the ancient times.

FIRST KANSAS

The first all-Black unit was not the famous 54th Massachusetts but the First Kansas Colored. This unit began to stand up in the summer of 1862 and in the fall of that year, these brave men distinguished themselves as a fighting unit at Honey Springs. Their first skirmish was at Island Mound, in Bates County, Missouri in October 1862.

This marks the First Kansas Colored as the first African Americans to see battle, and the first to die in action. A detachment of 225 men of the First Kansas Colored faced 500 Confederates. Ten were killed and 12 wounded, but the Confederates were driven off. The regiment's first taste of action had been a success.
This regiment was recruited primarily by James Henry Lane, without federal authorization, and against the wishes of the Secretary of War. Recruiting occurred across eastern Kansas in areas full of former or runaway slaves from Missouri.

The First Kansas Colored was officially attached to the Department of Kansas in June 1863. The Regiment was ordered to Baxter Springs in May 1863, and they bounced around Missouri. This was a test to see if African American men could be trusted with weapons, and if they had the courage and discipline to actually engage in combat operations.

The Battle of Poison Springs, 18 April 1864 was fought in Ouachita County, Arkansas as part of the Camden Expedition. The First Kansas Colored was positioned between the Union supply wagons and the Confederate lines. The First Kansas Colored repelled the first two offenses but ran low on ammunition and were beaten back by the third attack.

The Confederates refused to take the wounded black Soldiers as prisoners, and instead, brutally killed, scalped, and stripped them. In all, the regiment lost nearly half of its numbers. Estimated casualties were 301 and only 114 for the Confederates. Poison Springs is infamous for the Confederate's slaughtering and mutilating of these black U. S. Soldiers of the First Kansas Colored.

The First Kansas Colored is credited with participating in the battles of Island Mound, Cabin Creek, Honey Springs, Sherwood, Prairie Deanne, Jenkins Ferry, Camden, and Poison Springs.
In formation collected from the research of Ms. Lisa Hecker May 2015 and Wikipedia.

RETURN OF A HERO
– PTSD BAGGAGE

I'm back or at least a part of me is home!
The part that survived, the part that cries,
out for the old me.

The me I will never be again.

Not for you,
Not for my lover,
Not for my country, family, or friends.
PTSD is a killer of warriors,

Poets,
Moms,
Cousins,
Uncles,
Dads,
Children,
and frenemy

Who amongst you has not suffered,
Some type of stress or traumatic event.

Who has not cried, suffered, or been afraid?
Who has not wanted to belong and to not be rejected?
Felt neglected, lost a little hope, or played the fool.

I tell you the truth…you may have suffered alone but you survive in
a group, Living through poetry, surrounded by love!

REST EASY

When you come to a poetry event or if you listen to the news, you may hear that America is:
Racist,
Sexist,
Loaded with gentrifiers and hypocrites,
Full of liars,
Sexual predators.

You may hear that Americans are lazy, homophobic, and bullies.
But baby, what you will not here is that America is full of cowards or that these stars and stripes are scared of a fight.

Respectfully, here are the facts
America has the best trained, equipped, ready, deployable, and led military on earth and then we have lots of friends.
Just because you are feeling yourself while you are attacking a smaller less equipped country, please do not get things confused or out of order. If you step to the United States of America in war, I promise you, yes heed the warning, that someone else will raise your sons and daughters.

LIFE AFTER BEING A SOLDIER

Shaving – optional
Hair – flexible
Clothing – versatile
Pay – increased
Work hours – decreasing
Sleep – still minimal
Run – less
Stress – reduced
Travel – occasionally
Meetings – just as boring
Leadership – still demanding
Weight – increasing
Physical Training – If I feel like it
Work hours – set
Personal impact – diminished
Respect – generic
First names – with everyone
New world, new language, new concept, new pace, slower results.
Still living.
Retired Soldier!

WHY WE ARE GREAT

Real Talk

You are so blessed
As you are protected by the best.

This country is defended by the greatest and most capable military on earth and in history.

Here are three reasons why the U.S. military is the best, head, and shoulders about all others.

First, we have phenomenal leadership, and we study everything. The backbone of this military is bolstered by a Non-Commission Officer Corp (NCO) that is better than any ever seen. Other nations have tried to copy this NCO Corps, but they have all failed. The NCO Corps and exceptional leadership are the reason why we are great.

Second, the United States military fights as a combined force. When the might of Army, Navy, Air Force, Space Force, Marine, and at times Coast Guard come together, no nation can withstand this power. Also, the United States never fights alone. Before every fight and to ensure we protect them in their times of need, a coalition of allied partners is established. Called the Pacific Pac, United Nations, or North American Treaty Organization (NATO), just know, we never fight alone.

Third, all of that is overshadowed by the fact that we fight for each other. Fighting for each other has proven to be more powerful than fighting for a flag or even freedom. The United States military has an all-volunteer force that fights, lives, and trains like a family. More importantly and dangerous for our adversaries is, we never leave a member behind. That means we will not only come back for our fallen, we, will come back for those that hurt them. And if you hurt our family members, God help you because we will not stop until someone else is raising your children and the children of those that support you.

Because of these three things, one, phenomenal leadership and an outstanding NCO Corps, two fighting as a combined force and with coalition partners, and finally fighting as a family who never leaves anyone behind, we are the best ever.

Finally, we honor the rule of war which states "The strength of the Soldier is the team, and the strength of the team is the Soldier!"

This is why they are the best.

CHAPTER FOUR

Let's Grow Poetically

RULES TO SPIT

Yes, there are some basic rules if you have a poem to transmit.
Try to stay within these simple guidelines when you attempt to spit.

Title any poem you create.
It is a poetic crime to leave a poem nameless for heaven's sake.

Without a title, all you have are words on a sheet of paper similar to
an eye chart.
Name your work so you can at least tell your poems apart.

Next, make your point, and then let it go when you spit.
There is nothing worse than a poem that just will not quit.

Three to four minutes maximum for any poem you may write or
recite.
Our attention spans are short, so keep poems down to digestible and
chewable bites.

Be consistent with your writing and follow any pattern you set or make.
Spell check is not editing, so have your poems reviewed, and correct
any mistakes.

Do not use words you cannot pronounce and make sure to use them
in the correct way.
Some people are actually listening to every word that you say.
Follow the rules expressed by the host when you sign the list to sing
or read.
If you are told to do only one poem, it is extremely rude to read two
or three.

Please consider your audience and try never to offend.
Taking ten minutes to introduce a poem could be underestimating them.

Be clear so people can understand your words.
Speak up so you can actually be heard.

All writers are not speakers, and all speakers should not sing songs.
If you recite, practice your poems until you cannot get them wrong.

Yes, you can read from paper or an electronic device,
but if you want to be a spoken word artist, then from memory you may need to recite.

Now, find a spoken word event or poetic radio call-in-show to recite what you write.
Follow these simple rules the next time your name is called to take the open mic!

FREE TO SPEAK

I never heard a poem I did not like,
but I have heard some poems I would not write.

I once heard a poet say, "there is no poetry where I come from."
Now I realize everything is poetry that's my new rule of thumb.

Spend a day in the company of poets & by accident you can gain
more knowledge, than most individuals receive in one week's worth
of college.

Poets, writers, and deep thinkers all lend me your listening devices,
your ears.
For I have some poetic mandates you must hear.

You poets, you do not have the right to remain silent while at an
open MIC.
Someone needs to hear you spit, some soul needs to feed off you're
in-sight.

The day you first called yourself a poet you started your love affair.
But then you had to embrace your gift to create and your obligation
to share.

You may bless others with your poetic gifts in other ways,
I insist.
Produce CDs, publish books or just sign the open MIC list.

You have the right to speak to attorneys, doctors, politicians, or advisors.
Speak to lovers, haters, criminals, ministers, parents and even professors.
You have the right to shape minds and impact harden hearts.
You are called to dispel myths, use double entendres, and appear smart.

But if you do not wish to speak for yourself, how contrite.
The government will appoint another poet to speak for you tonight.

See, the poet is from heaven sent; use words to invent; Thoughts to prevent; you from missing a blessed event; your feet are not in cement. Take the MIC and represent, Remember - Silence is consent!

SEE THE POETRY

Do you know what your eye color actually means?
Everyone has eye color ranging from black, brown, hazel, blue, gray, or green.
Here is some eye color knowledge with a few generalities
I will tell you what your eye color says about your personality.

Gray eyes mean you portray deep internal strength, not generally affected by external pressures, you are more sensitive, and you have the capacity to manipulate yourself in accordance with your environment.

Black eyes mean you are extremely sensuous and very secretive. It is an uncommon color, and you are not great at sharing things about yourself or your life with others, so you are generally not a poet and I have little to say about you because you do not share much.

Hazel eyes mean you have a lot of sensitivity and empathy towards other people, you are fun loving, usually beautiful and you tend to have extremely unusual relationships, but your relationships tend to be brief. You are different and love trying new and innovative things. You like taking chances and you will hardly ever shy away from accepting a challenge.

Green eyes mean you are spiritual in nature, creative, vibrant, and compassionate. You have long lasting relationships as you possess probably the most amount of love whenever you are in a relationship, and you are known for being incredibly good looking.

<u>Brown</u> eyes mean you are more grounded and not swayed by materialistic needs or behaviors. You tend to be close to nature, independent, kind, and mentally tough. You are also incredibly attractive, adorable and your aim is to make new friends. You love cheering others up; you are reliable and will do anything for people who are special in your life.

<u>Blue</u> eyes have been called the most beautiful eye color and they are known for being extremely good looking. They have long lasting romantic relationships and they like making others feel satisfied. Assertive, straight forward, full of life and an acute sense of observations.

So, try not to deny that you cry as you look high in the sky at a shy but sly guy wearing a tie who is your ally that flies by and waves goodbye, it's just a poetic vibe right before your colorful and beautiful eyes!

JUST WRITE

Are there any poets here tonight?
Are there any "Ink Heads" who live to write?
Is anyone here a prisoner to poetry, a person who writes to breathe?
A person who expresses feelings through ink. See, if you can identify with my positive think.
I get up early to write, then I stay up late to recite,
Researching facts because I want to be right. My goal is to improve your mental sight.
Yes, I wrote the rules to spit, but some poets did not even get it.
Does not matter because writing, I will never quit. I even speed write without a permit.
So, let these bars penetrate your ears and grip your socks. There really is no such thing as writer's block.
A true writer cannot be hindered from their passion. Open mics are where poets actually cash in!
Spoken Word started the human race. Writing gives you mental breathing space.
Poetry helps you to embrace, life's issues as we run this race.
Poetry allows the "Haves" and the "Have nots" to interface.
Let me check again, are there any poetry lovers in this place?

POETIC LAMENT

Welcome to my poetic laboratory.
Sit back while I tell you a story.

God formed every beast of the field and
every fowl of the air.
Read Genesis Chapter 2 because it is written right there.

God brought the fowl and beast to Adam to be named,
So, when you do not name your poems, you should be ashamed.

God felt like everything He created should be named,
And for those of you not naming your poems, I hope He does not
feel the same.

A name sets the poem up and then sets the poem apart.
Names identify a poem, so give your poem its identity from the start.

Who creates something without giving it a name?
Why paint a picture if you are not going to put it into a frame?

It is like having a paragraph on a sheet of paper
all by itself,
really, who is reading that? A book with no title remains on the shelf.

Even when a child is born, they automatically
get your last name,
half the work is accomplished so stop being lame.

LET'S GROW

WOW, you are smart enough to create a new poetic piece of art,
but you are not creative enough to name it and set it apart.

If it is that difficult and traumatic then let me offer some assistance,
just give your creation the name of your opening sentence.

Name your poems and give them life because it is smart.
Name your poems so you can at least tell them apart.

I am not trying to fight or have an argument,
that is why I wrote this issue in my poetic lament.

RESPECT THE MIC

Want to know something I just do not like?
When poets talk while another poet is speaking at the MIC!

You would think poets would know better
You would think they would respect others reading their letter

When you know better you do better, I thought
They do not listen and during poetry they just talk

How could a writer disrespect the MIC?
Is it the poet or the poem you loath or just do not like?

How can a poet heckle a host during the show?
Causing confusion with their infusion to the poetic flow

It is like a crime you are committing on yourself
Not listening is destroying your poetic wealth

It resembles self-hate while others are listening to the lecture
You reek like a cannibal, maybe you are Hannibal Lecter.

Poetry neglector, Truth deflector, In court objector, Distraction reflector, Unwanted injector

As a host, I am a poetry protector
Now, respect the MIC your poetic disrespect-er!
You know who you are!

SPOKEN WORD

Have you heard about spoken word?
Do you believe in the power of poetry?
Do you know how to make words flow?
Can you spit words like a boss, in order to get your thoughts across?
Spoken word is therapeutic, it is like medication, and it takes a dormant mind and inserts stimulation.
It can relieve frustration and open lines of communication. Spoken word moves you to a higher mental station.
You can learn to use words and not ammunition to accurately state your position.
This could improve everyone's condition.
I hope you are open to this transmission, as you consume these words from my composition.
Please listen to every word that is said.
Chew on them collectively and let these words rest in your head.
Go over them again while you are in bed.
Write your own words so they may be read.
Do not let any truths go un-said.
This could keep future generations from being misled.
Now can't you see the power of poetry, the wonder, the knowledge, and the energy it can be?
The happiness, the love, and the life it can breathe can all be yours unconditionally, if you only take the time to believe in poetry.

POETRY CLUB

Everybody in the spot was spitting poetry,
    Truth is,

some of you really do not need to be.

Until your subjects and your verbs start to agree.
    Because

all you are doing is confusing me.

You are miss pronouncing words repeatedly.
Sounds like you cannot even read.

Spit that poem right and you will see.
There will be no one in the spot
as hyped as me.

BARS

I have forgotten more bars than most have written.
Start by sitting.
Give me all you've got baby, and I will still be spitting.
So, does Mr. Speaker have bars tonight? Darn right!

See, I am a hard hitter
Head splitter
Constant spitter
Seldom quitter
Spoken word transmitter.

Ask the people and you will see,
I spit educational bars, continuously,

Spilling ink, killing trees,
Delivering hope and liberty,
Uplifting spirits, get off your knees,
Mentally – not sexually,
Stand up straight so you can breathe

Close your eyes and see,
Colors, love, joy, honestly,

Read between the lines and actually,
Right their baby is where you will find the best poetry.

THE POET IS

A storyteller
Reporter
Singer or producer
The seer
The comedian
The writer and sometimes the fighter
The voice that cries out
An Artist, an emotional being
Revolution igniter
The poet is truth and perspective
The gay and straight
Feeling healing and myth creator and killer
Poets are movements
Healers, your help
They are both right and wrong
Anyone who wrote, produced, scored, or sang a song
Poets are love and hate
Yin and yang
Reasons and justice
An actor or the audience
Life and death
Professor and teacher
Preacher, minister, bishop, apostle, priest, atheist,
any religious leader
The rich or the poor
Sight, vision, and listener
Poets are creators
So, God, is the greatest Poet ever
Poets are light,
We are poets

CHAPTER FIVE

Grow Historically

BLACK HISTORY

So, you really want some black history, to see past the racial mystery.
Ok, listen to me, so you can understand what is clear if you study.

First there was darkness and then came the light.
Initially there was the black man and then came white.
Many times, ignorance precedes insight.

Black history actually got its start in Africa long ago.
We came through slavery not from slavery, so now, let's grow.

In 700 AD when the Africans Mores came to Europe and conquered
Spain, they brought astronomy, chemistry, physics, and geography.
They brought arts, mathematics, palaces, and literacy literally.

At that time, Europeans were 99% illiterate as they could not read,
so the Africans brought paper, books, philosophy, and universities.

They brought agriculture technology, apricots, figs, ginger, and dates.
Introduced Europeans to foods such as oranges, lemons, peaches,
sugar cane, and pomegranates in order to improve what they ate.

Cotton, silk, and rice where also introduced to these European peeps.
Africans also developed sidewalks and paved those dirty European
streets.

Africans introduced public baths, streetlights, and compasses to give
Europe some direction and to get them on the right page.

These African contributions to the world brought Europe into the Renaissance and out of the Dark Age.

So, miss me with Black History that started after we were slaves. Ancient Black History educated the people, cleaned them up, brought Europeans to their feet, and out of those caves.

WHO WAS THE FIRST

Tribute to Amiri Baraka

Who was the first to be taken?
Who was the first to be tricked?

Who was the first to be deceived?
Who was the first to be shipped?

Who was the first to die while afloat?
Who was the first to be thrown over the boat?

Who was the first to make it to this new land?
Who was the first to be sold on an auction stand?

Who was the first to be raped?
Who was the first to be called that word that rhymes
with bigger?

Who was the first to be beaten?
Who was the first to be killed by the taskmaster's trigger?

Who was the first to suffer castration?
What country taught Hitler all about discrimination?

Who was the first to deal with family separation?
Who was the first to die from a false allegation?

Who was the first to be freed, got the right to vote, and the right to purchase land?

Who was the first to be educated, truly appreciated, and treated like 100% of a man?

Who was the first to suffer from mutilation?
Who was the first to be denied graduation?

I do not know the answers to the questions I posed to you.
I wonder how our forefathers would feel if they knew your voting rights went unused.

Sometimes, it is hard to get people to face this,
but the freest country in the world just might be the most racist.

NAKED

Many have asked me, what is Critical Race Theory?

I will tell you that Critical Race Theory is Naked History,
No lies, no distortion, no fluff or fillers, and trust, it's not
a thriller,

See, we know how it ends. But for years, we have been deceived.
Tricked, bamboozled, confused, and told to believe - lies.

Critical Race Theory is the naked, untaught truth about American
history.
Running from facts is as crazy as trying to catch artillery,

rounds, so stay with me, learn something, do not be offended.
Remember, the truth is right, and it does not need to be defended.

Facts, Columbus landed in the Dominican Republic, three times
– Lost.
No one cares if George Washington lied about cutting down a cherry
tree but
You should know that Henry Boyd created the first modern bed.

Benjamin Montgomery invented the steamboat and
Thomas Jennings invented the dry cleaners. All black men but this is
not taught in schools.

If you faced the naked truth, then you would realize there is no way
a white male slave owner created finger licking good fried chicken.

He stole it – do not be fooled.
Critical Race Theory will show you that all these facts and many
more were mis-taught to us in American schools.
Teach the raw naked truth first,
or the internet will expose your lies which is much worse.

Look, tell the naked truth, be real, it is not that clever.
Life is short so write a naked poem that will last forever.

MUSIC TRANSITION

When did we lose it and where did we actually go wrong?
How on earth can we degrade our women through song?

Poetry tells it like it is, that I understand.
How are we going to move forward if we are degrading our women?

I believe in our freedoms as I fight for them every day,
but there are some things you just should not say.

Writers, poets, leaders, men of valor, lend me your ears.
We have got to stop degrading our women just to make money and hear cheers.

There is a place for hard core music and gangster rap if you need to get your points across.
We need to leave our women out of those lyrics before another generation is lost.

If you see a woman who is down on her luck or who is out to make a quick buck,
do not add to her problems, maybe you can help her get unstuck.

No other group of men degrade their women through songs.
This is the one area where we have gone wrong.

I am calling all you men to your position of leadership.
View all women, good or bad, as a vessel of God's workmanship.

If you do not have the capacity to help them out or get them home,
then do what you can, say a prayer, or just leave them alone.

MONIKERS

Deceiver, Kidnapper
Separator, Enslaver
Murderer, Colonizer

Rapist, Degrader
Master, Overseer
Castrator, Sex Offender

Child Molester, On the spot Executer
Religious Manipulator, Human Trafficker
Gentrifier, Domestic Terrorist

Timothy McVeigh, Jeffery Dahmer
Ted Bundy, KKK
Southern Crusader, Nazi

Anti-Muslim, Proud Boy
The Base, Anti-Jew
United the Right, Anti-Black

Daughters of the South, Anti-LGBTQ
Willie Lynch, White Supremacist

Anti-Civil Rights, White Nationalist
Racist, Insurrectionist

Complicit
American
Good people are not staying on this list. Once you know better, do better.

WHEN MY GRANDFATHER WAS YOUNG

When my grandfather was young, blacks could be lynched on an accusation with assistance from law enforcement.

My grandfather witnessed home-grown terrorism as whites legally lynched blacks in order to take or steal their lands.

During my grandfather's youth, 200 anti-lynching bills were introduced in congress but only THREE passed the House.

My grandfather lived through the movement of 1.5 million African Americans from the Jim Crow
South to the North in what is called the Great Migration.

My grandfather actually owned his own business in the South.

He was the bread winner, provider, Alpha male, leader, and a real man. He was grinding so much that his son's missed many of his lessons.

Missing those lessons allowed our people to stray and our values to drop. Our music went down, relationships suffered, and little girls struggled all because they needed, pops!

Study your history so you do not repeat lessons you should have learned. Some individuals are not moving forward which is my major concern.

The high school dropout rates are lower now than they have been in many years.

We have to keep the pressure on and help these young people find productive careers.

We all need to come together so we can move forward as one united people hand in hand.
If not, we could be a united people speaking a different language while being ruled by a foreign
regime in another land.

FROM THE EYES
OF MY FATHER

When my father was a boy, he had to ride in the back of the bus, he could not eat at certain restaurants, and segregation was the law in the south.
My father could not use just any bathroom, he could not go to just any school, and he had to sit in the balcony at the movie theaters.

When my father was growing up, he could not live in just any neighborhood, drink from just any water fountain, appear on television, his education was substandard, he was subjected to only jobs in the service industry, and he was unlawfully prevented from voting.
Back in my father's youth, Jim crow laws told everyone that blacks and whites could not even play cards, dice, dominoes, or checkers together. During that time, white and black prisoners could not even be handcuffed to each other.

When my father was young, black barbers could not serve white women or girls and a black man could be killed for looking or talking to a white woman. Violence was acceptable as a means to keep blacks in check. This is how it was when my father was young.
Back in my Father's Day, whites and blacks could not date or marry, and black men could not even shake hands with white men.

See, when my father was young, he lived in a slightly different America than we know today. Chances are, my, father grew up with your parents or grandparents in this the land of the brave.

Did your people march on Washington? Did anyone you know ever protest against injustice? Do you know of anyone who stood for what was right and against what was wrong? Maybe privilege has blinded you to the plight of others.

Have you ever seen a white man walk into a room where he was in the minority? Fear overcomes him normally, because of the things his father did to keep superiority. If he has the courage to stick around, then finding other white faces is his priority.

Truth be told, placed in similar situations, or given the same circumstances; we are all basically just alike. Power can corrupt anyone because it does not care if your skin color is brown, red, yellow, or off-white.
All have sinned, no one is perfect, and by God's grace, all of us are covered. Remember this when you think one group of individuals is superior to another.

Treat everyone with dignity and respect no matter what sex, race, sexual preference, religious belief or even the color of their skin. Because in the end, God is the only one deciding who wins.

MORALLY WRONG

Generally, two wrongs do not make things right.
Conflicts are not normally settled during arguments or forced fist fights,
and there are just some things you should not do even if you have the motive, muscle, or might.

Ponder a time or world where and when it was acceptable to be immoral and sin.
A place where evil men made lasting laws to win
because hateful, harden, harts control legal pens

The sly, slippery, sinister was allowed to minister,
as they use the legal system to display and administer, what they wanted.

Sample a few historical examples as we trample into this desperate deceptive ditch.

If a man was unhappy in his marriage and he immorally desired a switch,
all he had to do was accuse his wife of being a witch.

Marriage burned at the stake for his sake, and this allows his immorally clean break.
But wait, the evil within, continues to bind and bend as men covered their greedy sinful hearts with slavery.

Stay with me, rape, murder, child molestation, and sodomy along with other atrocities were covered by his greed and need to control while spreading his philosophy, seed, and democracy, religiously.

Then, evil hearts of women and men continued to twist and bend as they tried to ascend into the position of Him, who made even them as they tried to degrade blacks as being less then whole humans.

Legalizing sin causes miss-led hearts of women and men to never mend.
No healing as righteous remorseful repentance is pushed aside like bad friends.

Asking someone to seek forgiveness of a legal sin
is like asking a person to repent for driving,
through a green light, this is just not going to happen.

So, get strapped-in captain all around.
We are headed to the moral high ground.
Where right is right, and two wrongs are just wrong twice no matter what you do.
Do not ever let immoral individuals control you.

THE AGE OF HONOR

As immigrates migrated to America from Europe and
other places, they abandoned many things including
their language and familiar faces.

Many family traditions were maintained, and some you
can even read about in the Bible.
Europeans, Asians, and Africans all were somewhat tribal.

Tribes started in the Bible and continued in the new lands.
We may not call them tribes today, but we still like to cling
to our own bands.

In post-Civil War America, families became the new tribe or centers
of life.
They loved hunting, fishing, living off the land, and even killing
things with a knife.

Soon families turned to fighting each other as they created large
feuds or small wars.
Some of the famous feuds were the Lee's vs. the Peacocks, the Turks vs.
the Joneses, and the most famous was the Hatfield's vs. the McCoy's.

Many of these feuds were over pride, and to protect the family's
honor.
They disregarded the law, and they lived by street justice, as it was
stronger.

African American's development was about 150 years behind their Europeans peers,
due to slavery and institutional racism in the U.S. for hundreds of years.

Gangs such as the Community Resistance in Progress, also known as the CRIPS, along with the Bloods, took the place of tribes and families for African Americans in the modern hoods.

These gangs such as the DC Blacks, Philly Black Mafia, Mickey Cobras, and the Hidden Valley Kings,
along with the Black Guerrillas, and the Joy Row Boys, is where we found unity, love, and other things.

Gangs rule this world, all you have to do is look around and change their names.
The police are gangs, along with firemen, Congressmen, Soldiers, Marines, and even sports teams.

The age of honor is upon us as we live, breathe, and thrive.
All humans are basically the same because we all came from and cling to some type of tribe.

BLACK RIDERS

Horseracing is a glamorous sport, brought to the new world by the British.
Presidents George Washington and Thomas Jefferson frequented the track and in 1829 President Andrew Jackson actually brought his black jockey into the white house.

Racing was tremendously popular in the south, and it is not surprising that some of the first black jockeys were slaves. Blacks cleaned the stables, groomed, and trained some of the country's most valuable horses.

Black riders developed the abilities needed to calm and connect with thoroughbreds which are skills demanded of successful jockeys. Racing horses is the sport of Kings, but the rich were only spectators. Slaves initially and then the hired help took care of and raced the horses.

Many of the accomplishment of Black American horsemen in the early years have been all but forgotten. The first Kentucky Derby, held on 17 May 1875 had 15 riders and 13 of those riders were blacks and five of the trainers were black.

This initial race was won by 19-year-old black rider Oliver Lewis who road Aristide to victory. Two years later 17-year-old William Walker, another black rider claimed the Kentucky Derby. In 1892, black rider

Alonzo Clayton won the Kentucky Derby at the age of 15, making him the youngest person to win this race. Another 15-year-old black rider, James Perkins also won the Kentucky Derby in 1895. Willie Simms who won the Kentucky Derby twice, 1896 & 1898, and each of the Triple Crown races at least once.

Among the first 28 Kentucky Derby winners, 15 were black. James's "Soup" Perkins, who began racing at the age of 11, claimed the 1895 Kentucky Derby.

The most famous black jockey by far is Isaac Murphy, one of the greatest riders in all of American history. He is the first jockey to win three Kentucky Derby races (1884, 1890, and 1891). He won an astonishing 44% of all races he rode, and that record has not been approached by anyone since.

He is the first jockey, black or white, inducted into the Jockey Hall of Fame and he is in the National Museum of Racing, but he died at the age of 34.

Racing became a high-profile sport by 1921 and black riders were completely run out or reduced to being just stable help. Black riders even received death threats from the KKK and other racist to keep them from racing. The last black jockey to win the Kentucky Derby, was Jimmy "Wink" Winfield who won in 1901 and 1902.

Riders like Mr. Winfield went to Europe to continue their passion. He had a very lucrative racing career where he even road for the leader of Russia and retired with over 2600 wins to his credit.

Isaac Murphy, Willie Simms, and Jimmy Winfield have been inducted into the National Museum of Racing and Hall of Fame in Saratoga Springs, New York.

So, raise your mint juleps and toast to all the black jockeys of the past. These riders deserve far more recognition than they have ever received. Riders up!

THE TRUTH

(A brief history of Isabella {Bell} Baumfree AKA Sojourner Truth)

She was named Isabella Baumfree but gave herself the name Sojourner Truth.
They think she was born in 1797 but there is little proof.
She was born into American slavery, but with her daughter she escaped the owner's hands.
In 1826, she won her son's freedom in what is considered the first victory for a black woman in court against a white man.

She spit speeches off the top of her head or from her heart because equal rights for women was the plan. She is on the list of 100 Most Significant Americans of All Times by Smithsonian magazine and her most famous speech was "Ain't I, a Woman."

She was an abolitionist, a women's rights activist, and she was a trailblazer. She recruited black troops for the Union Army as nothing phased her.

She was from Swartekill, New York and she was born to James and Elizabeth Baumfree. Truth married a slave named Thomas, they had five children, and in 1799, NY started to abolish slavery.
In 1826, Truth escaped to freedom with her infant daughter, Sophia in the middle of the night.

Ms. Truth said, "I did not run off, for I thought that wicked, but I walked off, believing that to be all right."

In 1843, Truth became a Methodist and started preaching about the abolition of slavery and pacifism. Later, she expanded her fight for religious tolerance, women's rights, and against racism.

In 1850, William Lloyd Garrison privately published her book "The Narrative of Sojourner Truth: A Norther Slave." That same year she purchased a home and her speech at the first National Women's Rights Convention sent shock waves.

Even before the end of slavery, this brave woman was fighting for what was right. She was delivering speeches, helping people, while trying to take us to new heights.

Truth's grandson James Caldwell enlisted in the famous 54th Massachusetts Regiment during the Civil War. Later in 1864, she met President Abraham Lincoln, fought against desegregation, and much more.

She is credited with writing a song titled "The Valiant Soldiers," which is a song for the1[st] Michigan Colored Regiment. 1n 1870, Truth failed to secure land grants for former slaves from the federal government.
Sojourner Truth spoke about abolition, women's rights, prison reform, and against capital punishment. She died at her Battle Creek, MI home on 26 November 1883 but she and Harriet Tubman are remembered annually on 10 March for their accomplishments

SHOOK UP THE WORLD

Hands down voting closed
Best boxer ever, others exposed.

Because he floated like a butterfly,
And knocked other boxers to their knees.

A fighter and philosopher full of poetry.
Yes, I am talking about the greatest, Muhammad Ali!

Born 17 Jan 1942 Louisville, Kentucky that's right,
became a boxer because someone stole his brand-new bike.

Cassius Marcellus Clay, Jr., his given name, National Golden Gloves
and1960 Olympic Gold Medalist are some of his claims to fame.

He graduated from Louisville Central High School, the home of the
Yellow Jackets in 1960, not 63, and that
is where he got the slogan, float like a butterfly and sting like a bee.

19 and 0 with 15 knock-outs this was a man on a mission.
He became the top contender to the Champion Sonny Liston.

He beat Liston in Miami and became one of the youngest boxing
champions ever.
He defended his title every two months a tremendous endeavor.

He was too fast for Liston, too smart for George Frasier,
too cunning for George Forman and a political trail blazer.

At 25 he refused induction into the military; he would not fight.
He basically lost three years from his boxing life.

Twenty to twenty-five bouts missed, try to put that into perspective,
forget about the reason.
That is like not having Lebron James in the NBA for the last 4 seasons

Called the People's Champion and the Louisville Lip by some,
but outside the ring is where his best fights were won

Before Ali, we never heard a black man speak like this. Claim he was
the greatest and then had the skill to back it up with his fist.

The confidence, the swagger, the arrogance of this young black man.
Living in the segregated south with racial prejudice in the heart of
dixie land.

He showed us how to defeat your opponent before you entered the
ring. Confusing his thoughts, causing him to question everything.

Ali believed service is the rent paid for your room here on earth see,
and the Presidential Medal of Freedom and the President's NAACP
awards are what he received.

Social activist, humanitarian, philanthropists, champion no fuss.
Muhammad Ali is the proof that, we had greatness walking amongst us.

X

My father, Earl Little, was an outspoken Baptist Minister before I renamed him Earl X
He and my mother Louise Little gave birth to me in Omaha, Nebraska on 19 May - 1925 and I had 8 sisters & brothers

I guess you could say I inherited my civil rights activism and my ability to speak publicly from my father as we were forced to relocate twice due to death threats from white supremacist so the fight, the struggle, it did not start or end with me.

In 1931 they finally caught up with my father. They just left his body on those train tracks, but the police called it an accident along with the burning down of our home

That day, I lost both my parents actually, see my mother was never the same after pops was killed. She had an emotional breakdown not long after his death.

I graduated at the top of my junior high school class and would have been a lawyer if my teacher had not of told me that my career goals were not realistic for a nigger in the 40's.

With my dream shatter by my teacher, I turned to a life of crime. I was linked to robberies, prostitution, narcotics, and a gambling ring, well that is what they caught me doing.

With 8 sisters and brothers, I learned early in life, if you want something you had better make some noise and in Boston, I made noise. Arrested in 1946 for burglary with my may Malcolm "Shorty" Jarvis

10 years, damn, that's not a sentence judge, you gave me the whole book. White folk really did not like me robbing them, selling them drugs, and taking advantage of their women.

7 years I gave, I studied, I read, I self-educated, I rehabilitated myself to the point of enlightenment, see. I found the Nation or through my brother Reginald, the Nation found me.

WOW, those where the good old days. The Nation & the honorable Elijah Muhammad wanted empowerment, and to achieve political, economic, and social success. The Nation wanted a state of their own, separate from whites and I separated myself from the slave; name of Little. In 1952 I became Malcolm X.

Under my leadership, the Nation grew from 500 in 1952 to over 30,000 in 1963 all estimates, there were more of us and for some, that was too much power for anyone to have especially someone who looked like me.

Yes, my heart was broken when I discovered the discretions of the Elijah Muhammad and at that moment in my life, I began to question everything I had been taught.

Jealousy has always been a problem for our people and the Nation was no exception. Yes, I was silenced by the Nation and in 1964 I actually terminated my relationship with the Nation and formed my own organization, The Muslim Mosque, Inc., and I went on a life changing pilgrimage to Mecca which is in Saudi Arabia for some of you.

I learned that Muslim come in all shapes, sizes, cultures and most importantly all colors. I could no longer hate all blond hair and blue-eyed people as some of them were Muslim.

My message was now not directed at blacks only; my message was directed to all races and now my home, like my father's was firebombed on Valentine's Day 1965.

Haters pursued my father from Nebraska to Michigan until they finally killed him, and I knew my haters would stop at nothing until they got to me.

One week after the firebombing, in Manhattan, in Minister Louis Farrakhan's district, I was attacked by Muslim's I had taught, Muslim's I had trained, with Muslim approvals, under Muslim orders, hate and jealousy had taken over my Muslim brothers.

Shot 15 times by three gunmen in close range of my wife, 21 Feb 1965, 39 years old, I was gone before I left the room, gone before I was taken off that stage.

But did you see my funeral, now see, that was Muslim love. 1500 people attended my funeral! Friends, not grave diggers shoveled the dirt and buried me, more Muslim love.

I never saw the birth of my twin daughters, but my assassins, Talmadge Hayer, Norman Butler, and Thomas Johnson were convicted of 1st degree murder in March 1966.

Did you see Mr. Denzel Washington play me in Spike Lee's movie about my life, now that was love. I am gone but the movement is not forgotten. Yes, I made mistakes but who has not.

Let my life be a lesson to you that we should always seek truth, seek enlightenment, seek knowledge, seek understanding, and above all, seek love & you will find all.

THE FORGOTTEN BALLERS

Let me introduce you to some of the greatest athlete's racism tried to hide.
These ballers should have played in the Major Leagues, but they were denied.

So, they formed the Negro Baseball Leagues out of complete frustration,
while America dealt with a lack of understanding and Jim Crow's segregation.

All of these men are all-stars and the best at their positions,
and they played for the love of the game against any competition.

Center fielder, James "Cool Papa" Bell of the St. Louis Stars leads off this historic team with no shame.
He is known for being the fastest player ever, stealing 175 bases in only 200 games.

Batting second and playing second base, Martin Dibigo of the Cuban Stars (East), that is his name.
He is known for being the most versatile man ever to play baseball as he is an inductee in the Cuban, Mexican, and American Baseball Hall of Fames.

Batting third and playing first base, is the heavy hitting Walter "Buck" Leonard of the Homestead Grays.
He is named to a record eleven All-Star games and hitting home runs is how he got praise.

Josh Gibson of the Pittsburg Crawford's catches and bats cleanup with tremendous power.
He is famous for being the only man to hit a fair ball out of Yankee Stadium and over a couple of towers.

Batting fifth, playing left field, and managing is Oscar Charleston of the Indianapolis ABC's.
He is known for hitting like Babe Ruth, running like Ty Cobb, and actually managing the greatest team of all times to victories.

From the New York Lincoln Giants, batting sixth, and playing shortstop is Henry "Pop" Lloyd.
He is a clutch power hitter known for being a complete ball player all enjoyed.

Up next, a man with a very strong arm and quick hands, who is known for being the best third baseman to never make it big.
Batting seventh is the versatile baller from Newark Eagles, Ray Dandridge.

Christobal Torriente from the Chicago American Giants, bats eighth and plays right field because he is a notorious bad ball hitter.
This Cuban strongman hit with power, and he began his career as a pitcher.

The starting pitcher is a right-hander who is very colorful and known for being all the rage.
He is from the Trujillo All Stars and his name is "Leroy "Satchel" Paige.

The reliever, from the Chicago American Giants is Willie Foster, which is no mystery.
In the Negro Leagues, he is known for being the greatest left-hander in history.

Finally, Andrew "Rude" Foster, who managed the Chicago American Giants, is considered the father of the Negro Leagues, so he leads this team.

His strong personality and sheer physical presence allowed him to establish the Negro League and achieve his dream.

KARMA

Hello good people and poetry lovers. I am here to tell you that America has blood on its hands and blood all around its roots. Due to past actions, we are cursed to always need troops.

This country's founding four-fathers fled an oppressive class system then came to this new land and took the abuse of others to an even higher level. This, the land of the free was stolen from braves, built by slaves, and given to the rich!

This country has lied to, deceived, and vanquished Native Americans, was built off the backs of Africans from countries they did not conquer, and has mistreated every ethnicity known to man. America has blood on its hands.

I tell you that the Good Book states five times, twice in Exodus, once in Numbers, Deuteronomy, and again in Romans that God will visit the iniquities of the father upon the children to the third and fourth generation.

There is historic blood at America's roots and that is why killers target our school-age-children and why there is so much racial division in this great country.

America shows no remorse for kidnapping, enslaving, raping, lying, manipulating, human trafficking, and oppressing others and secretly subjugating women. Yes, I said it, the largest oppressed group in this country is women and many of them do not even realize it. If this is not true, then why is equal pay for women even an issue, why do we question a woman's right to choose, and why every time a woman runs for President, they lose.

This great nation will be pledged with producing small caskets and digging fresh graves until reconciliation is sought for immoral behaviors such as this:

On Sundays, white Americans would go to church to praise God, leave church, and go to a picnic where they would purchase and sell humans, then sexually abuse those adults and children, and finally, they would end the day with a good old fashion legal lynching.

What goes around, comes around as many do not live by the Golden Rule.
Trust me when I say, America has blood on its hands and at its roots!

Power corrupts and perceived absolute power has corrupted the moral character of this great country. America has sold its moral compass to the wealthy, and we have become nose blind to the stench of racism, sexism, classism, bigotry, and hatred while in pursuit of status and wealth.

The rich do not want you to have healthcare, equal pay, unions, a living wage, good schools, or control of your body. They have convinced many that these things are bad while they have them all.

I say, open your eyes, know this, sometimes to be silent, is to lie!

Mass shootings targeting children and innocent people has caused me to lament. I tell you now, this will continue until America repents.

UNTOLD HISTORY

It was not told that African sailed the world and spread their seeds long before Europeans.
Just check the color and features of the real people in India, Japan, Australia, America, and the Philippines.
It is not discussed that Africa was the center of the world, it just stays.

Research the Pangaea and you will see how from Africa, the other six continents just broke away.
Due to the dominance of African people, other tribes broke away and lived in caves. They did not vote for their leaders; physical power was the determining factor back in the day.

For millions of years, individuals lived in caves, shielded from the heat of the sun so they had to wear heavy things. With no sun, their skin, lighten and with no dirt, many lost their rhythm because they had limited connection to mother earth.

They also had to become more resourceful to survive. They not only had to hunt for today, but they had to prepare for the long winters, or they could die.

You may have never been told, but blacks dominated the earth long ago. Then complacency, greed, and deception eroded their power along with guns, bombs, and ammo.

It is not written that God separated the continents, but it is written that God did confuse the languages that we speak. This weakened Africa, divided their strength, and put them on a path for defeat.

Just check the most powerful nations today, which are England, China, Russia, America, and the Islamic States. They have one dominate language which enables them to effectively communicate.

If the African continent had one primary language, blacks would dominate the globe. We are still recovering from the sins of our fathers as these are some of the stories and facts that just go untold.

WHAT IF

I know many wonder "Why are black people persecuted so much in America?" So, let's grow.

On the sixth day of creation, God created man. On that day, man was given dominion and man had one vision and spoke with one voice.

Imagine if Adam and Eve walked this earth for thousands of years? What if the savior walked and blessed America long before He allowed anyone to move in?

Imagine if God created fear in order to keep you humble.
What if the foundation for all that you know and believe, was found not to be true?

What if everything you imagined came true?
What would you think of then?

What if we could use more of our brains, imagine what could you do?

Why would someone ever put the word "Good" in front of grief?

What if this pandemic came along to teach you to spread out, slow down, taste your food,
wash your hands, talk less,
listen more, honor the elderly,
see first responders, appreciate teachers,
respect medical people, love the ill,
listen to the vulnerable, clean more,

brush your teeth or deal with your own bad breath,
and smell the roses before you lose all.

Live now, life is short, and it could be over in a blink.
What if the only reason why this poem was written was just to make
you think?

GAME CHANGERS

None of these figures I am about to discuss should be
consider strangers. I am going to show you how these
four individuals were game changers.

The first game changer I want to tell you about could not
even see. That did not stop Ray Charles from changing the music
industry.

Mr. Charles was the first artist in history to maintain
ownership of all his master recordings.
You should have seen the record company
as they looked
at him like he was foreign.

Retaining his masters kept him in a position
to control all
the proceeds from his brand.
He was a game changer my people because
regarding his work, he took command.

Mr. James Brown is the next game changer, and it was not because
his style was unorthodox.
He changed the game because he was the first artist to tell the world
that we are the box.

That means he actually produced his
own shows, advertised,
sold tickets, and handle promotions.

He was the hardest working man in
show business because
he did everything while performing with
so much soul and emotion.

The next game changer was also in the music industry.
Michael Jackson was the first artist to actually purchase
a portion of a record company in music history.

Michael Jackson purchased 20% of Sony Records so he could control
things.
Most of you all just thought MJ could just dance and sing.

The last game changer is known as being
the mouth of the
south and the Louisville Lip.
Mohammad Ali told the world that he was the greatest as
he changed sportsmanship.

He was the first African American man to
tell a white man,
I am better than you.

Then he backed it up in the boxing ring as he beat his
opponents black and blue.

No one had ever heard someone arrogant and cocky enough to
predict the round he was going to win the fight.

Then get in the ring and back up what he said night after night.

These are just four individuals who thought outside
the box and changed the game. Sometimes the only thing you need
to do to hit a different target is to change your aim.

AMERICAN JUSTICE

Many of you have heard about Walter Scott, an unarmed black man, who was shot and killed by a police officer as he ran from that officer. The officer killed Mr. Scott while trying to administer a traffic citation. Mr. Scott never received the citation, nor did he make it to trial.

Many of you have heard of Eric Garner who was choked to death during an arrest for selling cigarettes which is a violation that he should have received a ticket. Mr. Garner never received that ticket, never made it to jail, and never made it to trial.

Many of you have heard of Miriam Carey, Michael Brown, Tyree Woodson, and Tamir Rice. All of these individuals where unarmed and killed by the police during their arrest. They did not live to stand in front of a judge.

Facts are, over 70 unarmed African American men and women have been killed by the police over the last few years. These individuals were not given due process, they did not receive their day in court, and many of the officers lied or covered up facts to prevent prosecution.

So why am I delivering these facts to you? Well, here is the other side of this story.

James Eagar Holmes, a white man, while carrying several weapons, gas grenades, and while dressed in tactical clothing, walked into a movie theater, killed 12 and wounded 70 people. After killing or injuring all these people, he was arrested by the police and taken to jail.

Timothy James McVeigh, one of the most famous American terrorist ever, killed 168 people and injured 600 others in one of the deadliest acts in U.S. history. He made it to trial.

Christopher Peterson, Jeffrey Dahmer, Charles Manson, Joel Rifkin, Dennis Rader, Richard Speck, Gary Ridgway, and John Wayne Gacy are all white men. They are all notorious American serial killers. They all made it to jail and trial.

This is why many chant "Black Lives Matter!" It does not matter how well armed they are or how many individuals they kill, a white criminal will make it to trial eventually

On the other hand, you do not even have to commit a criminal offense and some police officer will shoot a black man dead in the street. Check the facts because today, right now, on these streets right here, Black Lives Really Do Not Seem to Matter!

CHAPTER SIX

Grow In Love

BABY GIRL

I want to start a conversation with you that will last several generations. Our combination will bless nations, come feel the verbal vibration of our collaboration.

Me loving you through thick and thin to levels only God can comprehend.
I am not your father or your mother but baby, I am your biological lover.

Sweetheart, live this dream with me,
where the only thing better than us is pure fantasy.

Take this journey as poets write and live vicariously through what they see.

Come, lets join hearts, souls, lives, and hands.

Allow me to show you the strength of a submitted and committed man.

Be my life's diamond so that every time I see you, my soul slows down to admire your presence, your beauty, your essence, and your favor.

The day we join hands, I will forever savor.

When I listen to music, it is about us that I reminisce.
See baby girl, you are every song in my play list.

Be my spades and dance partner for life,

mutually covering one another, turn to me during strife.

Add to my confidence, be my good thing, and increase my abilities happily.

Your presence in my life is proof that there is a God and that He loves me tremendously.

I am standing here hoping to have a life-long conversation with you.

So, Baby Girl, with me, I would like to know, what are you going to do?

POWER COUPLE

You see them, you want to be them, and you may not even know why.
His clothes, her hair, his shoes, people do not care.

He is a leader, a shot caller, a check writer, and he is an alpha male.
She is a queen, diva, an inspiration, and she is on a simply higher scale.
Both are intelligent, wise, and well put together as they ride the rails.

As a power couple, you are always in the spotlight.
Strangers want to be your best friend on sight.
They set the bar high as a satellite, broke people are their Kryptonite,
their relationship is watertight.

They can make friends with enemies and not start a fight.
They are a power couple that's right.

Eyes and lies follow them,
Cameras smile at them,
The "In Crowd," yes, that is them,
Hater's plot against them,
Locals and lovers are inspired by them,
Stop, wait, look, you even listen to them.
Always in the spot, you know them,
Local celebrity, you know you are looking for them.

Heck, maybe you are them?
If not, get in line if you want to be them.
A power, couple?

CRAZY, SEXY, COOL (QUEEN)

She is crazy with laughter and passion,
Shows a sexy style through her fashion,
Such a cool demeanor that is filled with compassion.

No need to talk as her energy and face display her feelings.
Along with her beautiful smile that is so appealing.
The first time you see her it is amazing, the second time is confirmation, while the third time means determination.

She is loyal, hardworking, practical, determined, and kind.
Generous and easy to talk to if you want to relax or unwind.

Her friendship is awesome if it is granted, but remember her conversations are straight and not slanted.

She has handles, point guard skill, and her flow is out of sight, well, make sure she has had her vitamins, or she may not last half the night.

Her dominos game keeps improving,
But to me she keeps losing,
Regarding her education, she is not snoozing,
And while at work, she keeps it moving.

She is always on top of things.
In front or behind she controls the scene.

In my dream she reigns supreme my heart, my Queen.

ALL HANDS (TO BUTTAFLY)

Her hands are amazing to me.
Makes me want to go palm to palm to see,
how we match, how soft, how close, how lovely!
She looks like her handles could heal!

She is gifted with strong paws to cover other's disabilities.
Watching your back, covering your liabilities,
holding you down, her primary capability.
Adding maximum pressure is a major ability,
because she has been blessed to carry more responsibility.

If she tells you that she has got you, then she is clutch
and I believe her love language has got to be physical touch.
See, her grippers equip her to hold onto love.
And when it snows, be smart, get her the large gloves.
There is nothing about her or those fingers that is common, you
know, and I bet those hands could hold at least 11 dominos.

Her mitts match her heart, large, generous, and giving with four
chambers or parts. Those hands feel, hold, carry, and write. She claws
to be close to the light, that smile is such a delight, and her words
always bring insight.

But I digress, so let me redress my inner thoughts if I can.
The bottom line is, I really just want to hold your beautiful hands.

MAHOGANY

She is mahogany.
A visual symphony,
clearly high quality.

An orchestrated orchestra visually.
Put together and composed musically, yes strategically.
Carved cut and crafted expertly, not magically.

She is magnificent,
from heaven sent,
the perfect complement.

She is like water, oxygen, and land to the earth,
blue to the sky,
cotton to shirts,
she is dinner and dessert.

She's a sundress, not a skirt.

I hear music when she walks,
lyrics when she talks,
she is graceful like a hawk,
and she educates like chalk.

To me, she is a majestic tree,
on the beach in Waikiki,
stretching heavenly,
simply, she is mahogany!

BORN TO A FAMILY
OF SERVICE

(From a Soldier to a Nurse)

In the spirt of them that are sometimes called sister, healer, wet, or midwife.
It means to nourish, cherish, protect, and even save life.

In loving memory of Florence Nightingale, to Mary Eliza Mahoney, to Linda Richards, and Phoebe, the first in the Bible, nurses have always been the unsung heroes to healthcare.

This Soldiers truly appreciates, trust, and respects
the nurse.
I honor you, life protector, and natural nurturer with this poetic verse.

From your heart of love to your hands that give,
to your eyes that calms, back to your voice that fills,

the air with compassion as you interpret that medical grammar.
See, we all know nurses are there because doctors sometimes lack proper bedside manner.

Your professionalism, compassion, dedication, and commitment come first,
In the spirit of a RN, LPN, practitioner, ICU, and also the traveling nurse.

Even if you lack the proper personal protective equipment or gear.
You still take your positions on the frontlines and smile to your patients through fear.

You provide comfort and mercy to the dying with courage the faint of heart has not seen.
A nurse serves patients from the start of life to death and all that is between.

Because you prevent illness, help with coping, restore individuals, while promoting health.
All of this is accomplished with no fanfare and limited wealth.

What I know and believe to be true,
all this country stands for is seen daily
through nurses like you.

I thank God for blessing us with Nurse-Angels who will always be in my prayers.

You are appreciated for providing excellent and life-saving patient care!

THIRSTY

Chasing,
Mouse trap
Gotcha
Stop
Whipped,
Stripped,

Paying for romantic nights or trips,
Dodging relationship but wanting companionship
like you need cab fare, avoiding love everywhere
But need sex like footwear, healthcare, or just air.

The trapper, the pray,
The game,
Both get laid
One receives benefits, I mean gets paid.

Orgasm if you are not afraid.
Release, pull close, push away,
E-Cigarette for some,
cold water for others.
Round two, red bull for me then round three.
Ciroc on ice, the trap, equals great sex.
Getting Sexually bitten
Smitten, over time, not quitting.

There is a knock at your heart, trapped, cannot get away.
Companionship leads to sex, then love, all because your ass was thirsty.

WHERE IS THE LOVE

Built ford tuff, not manufactured.
My erection stands for your satisfaction.

Fine-tuned for your maximum attraction.
I'm chiseled for just your distraction.

And then your relaxion, well that is my goal and task.
So, sign this W-2 because I am about to work that ass.

Forward, back, up, and down.
Welcome to my climax class.

If you did not know before now you are going to learn.
Gag is not a reflex here and no words are safe.

This is no place for amateurs and
your body count matters.

Less than 10, do not bring your ass in,
I am not responsible for your corruption.

But you can get some sexual healing.
Bring your passion but do not catch feelings.

LOVE LETTER

Sweetheart, all I have is love for you, have no despair,
because you are as fine as frog's hair!

Listen as I speak your love language and sing your favorite song. You
have my complete attention and I have not even seen your thong.

Seriously, what I know and believe to be true,
the word beautiful was invented just for you.

I want to share countless intimate conversations with you.
I look forward to even more non-verbal communications with you too.

Your brains combined with my muscle,
together we instantly become a power couple.

Invincible, admired, hated, and envied all at
the same time,
Baby, take my hand as we start this climb,

to the top as you are my muse and my motivation,
your voice is my music, your smile is my inspiration.

You are my help, you give me strength, and
you give me peace.
Come share my life and watch our love and
blessing increase.

You are my song; you are my ink.

You are my flower; you've changed how I think.

So, let my words caress you as I get next to you.
It is my job to protect you and I will never neglect you.

Been in this wilderness 40 years, lost wondering all around the world.

God was perfecting me, training me, to recognize you, as my perfect girl.

UNDERSTANDING MEN - FATHER TO DAUGHTERS

Baby girl,

If he does not call, he does not like or value you.
If he does not keep his word, he does not respect you.
If he is inconsistent, you are not his priority.
If he only calls when he needs something, he
is using you.
If he starts random arguments, he has someone else.
If you have never met his family, you are a side piece.
If you have been dating for 5 years, you are a place holder.

Broke men want a woman to fix them.

Immature men want to be mothered or taken care of.

Lazy men want enablers.

Insecure men want puppets.

Abusive men want objects or property.

Jealous men want control or dominance.

Good men want partners.

Hard working men just need support or help mate.

Look, when a man loves a woman, she becomes his weakness.

When a woman loves a man, he becomes her strength.

Women want to be loved by the man they admire.
Men want to be admired by the woman they love.

God could have created you from any bone
in the man's body but he chose the rib.

You are to protect his heart, cherish his love, honor, and respect him.

Find you a man that you trust enough to get on his sheet of music.

Because this man will love you enough to let you sing.

WHAT A WOMAN REALLY WANTS

What does a woman really want, that is the question that was asked? Many times, she wants everything she just simply cannot have.

Like a pink elephant, a perfect body, or purple unicorn in flight. She wants a man that is handsome, great in bed, and he brings his six-figure income home at night.

I was just being funny while writing from inside this phone booth. She wants someone who is strong in convictions, keeps their word, and always speaks the truth.

She wants someone who speaks fluidly and confidently.
Someone strong enough to communicate her love language daily.

She is looking for a funny partner, thoughtful provider, and someone full of respect.
A person that sees, listens, honors, supports her strengths and her weakness he protects.

She never feels neglected because he shows and knows her worth. This person makes her feel like she is the only woman on the earth.

For him, because she is deeply loved, and he completes her dream. This person above all, treats her daily like a Queen.

PRENUPTIAL
HOUSE RULES

Since the time of Adam and Eve, the family construct has been under continuous attack from outside forces.
These battles have led to many divorces and several corpses.

Resolve all disputes before your close the chapter on that day. Respect each other and always honor the things you say. Honor yourself and your house and keep no secrets from your spouse. Everything must be shared, no secrets.

Before leaving, the departing person must kiss the individual staying at home. While the returning person should be greeted by the person who is at home with a hug and a kiss. Monthly date night should be planned scheduled and not missed.

Discuss the current issue without bringing up settled disputes or old stuff. Argue in privacy, never in public and during disputes, no one leaves.

Your spouse has 51% approval on wardrobe and friends.

No sleeping separately in the same house and have sex at least twice a week with your spouse.

Spouse gets reasonable doubt.

WEDDING VOWS

Today your team is set, and your body is whole again, as you are
reunited with your rib, and you are joined with your best friend.

Your life mate, better half, and partner in crime.
You must be all these things for each other to stand the test of time.

As teammates, you will encounter no obstacles you cannot overcome.
Today you are two who stand as one.

Together you will feel no rain,
endure all things,
form an unbreakable chain
cast no blame,
as you carry the same name,
while on love's campaign.

Always depart each other's presence with a hug and a kiss.
Return the same way to symbolize they were missed.

Together you will find no disagreements larger than thee.
You will witness no individuals who can divide your home I decree,
The end of this marriage one of you will never see,
As I pray this union last indefinitely.

POETRY AND LOVE

(Inspired by Smokey Robinson – Cruising)

Smokey Robinson sang - Music was made for love
While Mr. Speaker says poetry displays that love,
Feel the vibe when we come together.

Poetry was made for love
Reciting conveys that love
I love it when we are vibing together.

Poetry is my ride or die
Without it I cannot survive
I thrive through writing poetry baby.

Writing takes me from here,
Puts me in the atmosphere
I love writing verses for my lady.

Poetry was made for love
Reciting conveys that love
I love it when we are vibing together.

Do not leave the room my dear,
These verses you need to hear
I come alive while spitting poetry baby,

Let poetry help you unwind
Give in and you will find
There is nothing like poetry lady.

You've got things to say,
So glad we have poetry
Come release those verses baby

Poetry was made for love
Reciting conveys that love
I love it when we are vibing together.

ME AND POETRY

I made love with poetry last night and we produced poems, haikus, and limericks to dim light.

Felt so good as poetry held me tight until every line was just right.

Then poetry whispered, "Mr. Speaker, do not put me on a time clock because you know, there is no such thing as writer's block!"

So, I blocked and tackled that task, wrote until I mentally crashed.

See, poetry undressed me verbally, pulled me in physically so I gave her my words individually.

Poetry and I have had relations, two or three times daily as we be creating.

Poetry has me feeling emotions, hopes, and even aspirations so I keep producing every time I feel that verbal vibration.

Together, we move nations, educate generations, inform poetic congregations, during this collaboration and we end up having a poetic celebration.

With poetry, my thoughts are foreplay.

Putting ink to paper is like getting laid.

Typing in a computer or phone is an upgrade.

Then, I meet poetry on stage at an open mic to relax.
Me, poetry, and that mic equals a climax.

See, I slept with poetry all night, let me be clear.
I know poetry takes other lovers when
I am not near.

But that is alright.

So, ask me and I will give you some insight, because baby, I am
sleeping with poetry again tonight.

WHAT SHE SAID

An intelligent conversation with this successful woman was the game plan. Then she said, Mr. Speaker I do not need a man.

That's how it began, mental sparring, verbal jousting counter concepts conceived. Deceived by the deceiver, could I even make her a believer?

I am not addressing those that have and know they want a man.
I am addressing those that have said they do not need a man. Look, it is not that she needs him, or they need them, I defer. Baby, the fact of the matter is, he needs her.

He needs you, do not be confused or fall apart. Men have needed women from the start, of time, and we need you just as much today, stop any division.

We need advice on everyday decisions,
To keep us on mission, to validate our vision we need you like patients need physicians,
like military needs tacticians, like Quartermasters are true logisticians.
God knows, black men need women to help keep them out of prisons.

Most times, two heads are better than one. Phone a
friend, let him in, do not stop earning your wealth.

No one really wants to live, love, and celebrate life by themselves.

When your Bozas is not connected to you, he is a fraction of himself, forget the wealth, men are not built to be by themselves.

Queen, who other than your lover would honor and cover you and your crown like a spouse?
A home without a roof, is not really a safe or enjoyable house.

Please do not reduce marriage to a financial transaction.
When you say, "I do not need a man," you speak against God's plan.
Your words, a "Curse of Eve" reaction.

Not needing a man, distraction.

Showing little faith, fighting the laws of attraction.
as you cannot wait and ceiling your own fate.

Because you put those words into the atmosphere.
Hiding behind pride and now, no real man will even come near. What you do not need, is a person imitating a man, going half on dates, cannot keep fact straight or pull his own weight.

Do you know the power of the words you say? You speak and drive your blessings away. Always ask for and seek the best. Consider every word and thought as a prayer requests.

Make your money, do your thing Sweetheart, but remember what God designed you to do, because I promise, a man somewhere really, really does need you.

CHAPTER SEVEN

Grow Wiser

DEHUMANIZATION

Tactics, techniques, and procedures are used by the military to train individuals to fight and win wars, because defeating your enemy is how you survive a combat tour.

The military uses the procedure of dehumanization, so the 6th commandment Soldiers would break. Make the enemy less than human and their life is easier to take.

You brainwash service members, so they do not think that they are sinners.
Trick them in order to make them more effective killers.

Check it, the Indians were called savages, and the Japanese were called Japs. Muslims were rag heads, Somalians where skinnies, and the Germans well; we called them krauts.

Once dehumanization is taught, it is all downhill.
These Soldiers are ready, willing, and able to
score quick kills.

Efficient, effective, killing machines yes, that is right,
But what happens to these Soldiers after the fight.

You label black men as 3/5th a human which diminishes their worth.
You make lynching legal, raping acceptable, and you under educate them from birth.

You turn white Soldiers to police and use the media to frighten the masses. Listen and learn without looking at this through rose-colored glasses.

Cops do not always see black or brown citizens at traffic stops, this is not political. Through dehumanized eyes, police see rapist, drug dealers, thugs, immigrants, and un-convicted criminals.

Now you know why the United States leads the world in unarmed killings of people of color by cops. Understanding the police adopted procedure of dehumanization is the first step to correcting this, so the unarmed shootings can stop.

AN OPEN LETTER
TO THE PEOPLE

Regarding Police Shootings

We should stop holding beat-cops and junior policemen solely accountable for these shootings of unarmed individuals. That is like punishing drug users while allowing drug dealers to go free.

The police commissioners, senior police officers, and other top law enforcement individuals are responsible for the training of these officers, and they should be held accountable for their subordinate's actions.

When a police offices states "I shot because I was afraid," understand, that officer was not adequately trained.

When the first person in leadership is held accountable for the actions of their subordinates, you will start to see better trained officers patrolling our streets.
Little known fact, many of the officers involved in these shootings are let go by their police departments even after they beat their court cases.

Do you expect a district attorney to bite the hands that actually feed them their cases? Justice
does not reside there.

Police officers are professionals and should be held to a higher standard, not lower. Only the most responsible individuals should be put in a position to take lives. It seems that some police departments have lowered their standards and then the system enables them to get away with cold blooded murder.

Finally, we the people must make a stand. If they do these things to one of us, they can do these things to any of us. No jury in America should lower standards for individuals we have given our trust and confidence.

See, I know this because I am a Soldier. I am entrusted with the lives of our sons and daughters. I am held to a higher standard daily. America has placed trust in confidence in me and I am required to uphold a higher standard.

My people carry guns, and they are cleared to protect and defend but not kill due to fear and a lack of training.

We need to hold police officers to the high standards they signed up for when they put that uniform on, when they received those weapons, and when they recited that oath. Protect and Serve Everyone!

ABUSIVE RELATIONSHIP

Have you ever wondered why people remain in an abusive relationship? Harsh words, foul treatment, broken bones, bruised eyes, and busted lips.

From the outside looking in, you seem to always have the answers to this abomination.
Leave them, report them, fight back, but by all means, do not stay in that situation.

But from the inside of this relationship and to compensate, excuses are made.
They did not mean it, it was a miss understanding, I caused it, or they were just afraid.

Even as the victim hangs from trees, lays in caskets, or sits behind unjust bars!
We sing, we shall overcome but we have not, so stop the speeches and stop the seminars.

I woke up today to realize that we have been in a long-term abusive relationship.
A relationship where:

-The rules for them do not apply to me and they act like they do not realize this.

-I have helped make them what they are today but it is not appreciated.

-I do what they refuse to do, and they overlook me.

-There is no love, and little appreciation in this relationship.

-Everyday, I am mistreated, misunderstood, and depressed.

-I have been dealt all hearts in a game of spades!

The crazy thing is, I am the victim of my oppressors' fears. Yes, you fear me.
From the first time your father told you about me, you feared me.

When the black African Moors conquered European nations, you hated me,
as the Egyptians studied, educated, and ran the world, you plotted against me.
Then you used my brother to capture me, you chained me, beat me, enslaved me, raped me, refused to educate me, and resented me because you still were not better than me.
Now police use fear as a reason to indiscriminately kill me.

Then you passed laws to hold me down.
Lost a war and invented jim crow laws to maintain an advantage,
then from vigilante justice through lynching,
to stop and frisk, to stand your ground, now this.
Full circle, legal public lynching caught on video.

Let me school you right here! See, slave owner, well they are rich and do not always recognize privilege or racism because that is like oxygen to them.

But the old overseers, poor white individuals, disenfranchised whites, sometimes called trailer trash or other derogatory names, they are the ones who worked overtime to keep minorities down while pretending to hold themselves up. Rich equals slave owners, some beat-cop equal overseers.

Mine eyes have seen the coming of the destruction of America from sea to sea and town to town.
Through this wedge that divides, your racism is the old boot used to hold new black necks down!

What is the black man to do? If he runs, you kill him.
If he holds his hands up, you shoot him.
If he stands and does not resist, you choke him out!
What do you expect to happen next?

Now that he, I, we have reached our breaking points, been demoralized, discouraged, dishearten, filled with complete dismay, and frustrated. Answer this, what comes next? Even a coward can find the nerve to fight when left no other options and trust me, I am far from a coward.

My pen cuts all you that are starting smoke.
You will show up to loot, but you will not show up to vote!
If the shoe fits you, are a disrespectful disgraceful joke.

Black hands help build this land. No American wars have been won without the black man.

Hispanics, Latinos, once they have killed me, you must know you are next on their hit list. Then the Jews, Asians gays and anyone that does not look like Hitler.

This country values success over justice and trades compassion for condonation.
Lower your voices, putdown your torches, holster your weapons and have a simple conversation.

No, sadly, this will not be the end to all our adversities,
but America, when will you realize that you will never be great without true diversity!

KILL-O-THERAPY

Kill-O-Therapy otherwise known as Chemotherapy in the medical field, is the primary treatment for cancer patients and how they are healed.

Chemotherapy kills cancerous cells that rapidly divide,
all in an effort to help the cancer patient survive and remain alive.

Unfortunately, chemotherapy also kills
perfectly good cells.
It kills everything it contacts, and it actually poisons the body as well.

This treatment could save your life and even make your body cancer free, while causing you to lose your hair, weight, appetite, and the feeling in your extremities.

Millions of dollars are donated annually for cancer research, I am sure. We have some of the smartest individuals in American and we still have no cure.

Kill-O-Therapy actually shows our ignorance of cancer and the ways it spreads.
Chemotherapy does not always work, and some cancers grow until the host is dead.

Cancer respects no one, it does not matter who you are, how poor or how wealthy.
30% of cancer related deaths can be prevented with immunizations and living healthy.

Here as some facts, you can take with you:

- There are 100 different types of cancer that could affect any part of your body.
- Cancer is 13% of all deaths worldwide – about 7.6 million in 2008
- Top 5 killers for men: lung, stomach, liver, colon, and esophagus cancer
- Top 5 killers for women: breast, lung, stomach, colon and cervical.
- Tobacco use is the single largest preventable cause of cancer in the world – 22% of cancer deaths.

The best approach is to detect early, treat adequately, and avoid smoking for sure.

If you must, use chemotherapy until cancer researchers come up with a better cure.

THE UPSIDE TO CANCER

Death is coming for all of us, no matter how healthy
you are or how much you work out. Death respects
no one as you will leave this place and that is no doubt.

My mother taught me to look for the silver lining no matter how bad
the storm or your level of sorry. Just like the thief crucified with the
Savior, any of us could be in heaven tomorrow.

When death comes from cancer it is generally bad news because it
destroys so much.
Cancer eats away at the physical, but the spirit, it cannot touch.

I am not celebrating cancer so do not take this the wrong way. Cancer
still destroys, kills, and send loved ones to early graves.

There are many issues with cancer that we must deal with off the top.
Alzheimer's disease takes your memory while heart attacks make your
blood flow stop.
Any of us could die in over one thousand different ways or even in
our sleep, not to mention.

Here are some upsides to cancer I want to bring to your attention.
Cancer gives you space, cancer gives you grace, cancer lets you know
you are leaving this place. Cancer allows you time to get things in
order and it gives you time to let your daughter know, you love her.

Cancer gives you the opportunity to say goodbye, I will miss you,
and I am sorry if I was not polite. Cancer allows you the opportunity

to say thank you, write a Will, or seek forgiveness as you set things right.

With cancer, you have a chance to say things you may not have had the chance if you were hit by a bus. Cancer gives you time to stop, assess your life, and if necessary, adjust.

It allows you to be visited while you can still be heard.
Cancer allows you to hear your son's final words.

Cancer is an indiscriminate killer with no respect for who we are or how much money is in your purse. Cancer can even give you time to meet a wonderful hospice nurse.

We are all going to leave this place no matter how healthy, how wealthy, or how wise you may be. Take advantage of the space cancer gives to get things right and heaven will be the next thing you see!

HOW THEY SEE ME

As a baby, when I stood with my hands up, my mother would pick me up and show me some love.

When I stand with my hands clasped together, I am speaking with my Savior.

When I stand in my uniform and salute, I am greeted and respected by those associated with the military.

When I stand with both my hands above my head, well this is how the police want to see me, because even like this, I am resisting arrest.

When I pose to the left to get my picture taken at the station, the judicial system is happy because this view makes them profitable.

When someone places my hands upon my chest as I lay in rest, well this is how some want to view me because I am no longer a problem or a mince. Now, I am a good black man, dead.

But baby, when I stand before a mic, I stand in defiance of Jim crow, racism, segregation, & bigotry.

When I graduate, I overcome institutional barricades.

When I mentor others, I honor my ancestors.

When I raise my children, I break generational curses.

LET'S GROW

When I show up, I dispel some stereotypes.

When I study, I show myself to be approved.

When I use proper English, I am mocked.

When I get paid, I am hated and envied.

Seems like the more hate some have, the more negative things they project onto me.

But when trouble comes, I am sought after, relished, and wanted.

When times get hard, I become your best ally and friend.

So, when you see me do this, it means rally on me and when I do this, it means follow me.

See, when we find our way, we are the best categorically.

So which version of me and this country do you see?

WHEN YOU WALK WITH A LIMP

When you walk with a limp, people tend to stare, and I have to pretend that I do not see them and that I do not care.

When you walk with a limp, nice individuals show concern and compassion almost as if they can feel your pain while others pay little attention and sometimes, they show complete distain.

When you walk with a limp, some people even feel compelled to let you know it as you stole by, as if you cannot feel the discomfort with every stride.
I walk with a limp when I rise from sitting for a long time or after chilling with comrades.

My limp actually gets worse as the weather gets bad.
See, I walk with a limp so much I do not even realize it now. I just keep moving, keep rolling, keep writing, and I keep growing because nothing is going to hold me down.

My limp may be visible to you while I am moving about and do my thing. Some of you have other elements you are able to hide and keep unseen.

I appreciate your concern and I appreciate your compassion but please do not let my limp be a distraction.

As an athlete, sprinter, and Soldier with an active lifestyle, I hurt my knees being all I could be. The doctors told me to stop running, I did not, and that lead to multiple surgeries.

I should have been more careful with my physical fitness back in the day. Just for the record, my limp does not prevent me from accomplishing anything and it does not keep me from getting paid.

Thanks for your concern and for your thoughts because your compassion fills my cup. I am blessed by God, so I will keep moving and I suggest you figure out how you are going to keep up!

THINGS MY MOTHER WOULD SAY

Let your food stop your mouth.

What do you think I am doing, eating paper, and shitting money?

One monkey don't stop no show.

Stop and smell the roses.

To be early is to be on time.

You better eat everything on that plate.

Your eyes are bigger than your stomach.

My momma did not raise no fool.

Your daddy wasn't a glass maker.

I will knock the taste out of your mouth.

You can be or do anything you want.

Be in before the streetlights come on.

Do you want to play pokeno.

Let's go on a bear hunt!

I brought you into this world and I will take you out!

QUESTIONS FOR MOMMA!

Momma, I have a few questions before we go to sleep tonight, would you please tell me why is my skin so light?
Why do not I have skin as dark as the night and tell me, why are my eyes so bright?

I am asking you out of love as you are my primary teacher
why do I seem to have so many white features
Momma, why do some white people look at us in such a strange way.
You know, like they are afraid of us or like we are runaway slaves.

Why do people here harbor so much deep-rooted hate. Why does racial, sexual, and religious differences still divide these United States.

Why is the daily news filled with so much violence and drama and please tell me why so many citizens hate Presidents Bush and Obama?

Why does the United States have so many serial killers on file? And why do we have so many sexual deviants and pedophiles?

When did we officially lose our original last name? Do you know from where we actually came?

Are you telling me I will never know, and my past is just a mystery? Is that why there are very few positive things written about black history?

Momma, I am not trying to press you or hurt you see that's not my task but there are a few more questions I just have got to ask.

Why does the United States fight for freedom and then harbor so much racial mess? Why does the United States send billions overseas while citizens starve right here take a guess?

Why is there so much hate towards interracial love and dating? Why do Americans immigrants, look down at others who are still migrating?

Why do we have so many people in prison lead by black men? Why do poor people without health insurance oppose the President's health care plan?

Why do millions smoke when they know it kills them and their friends? Why do so many father's walkout on their families without paying dividends?

Why do so many mothers seem to kill their own seeds? And why do so many young girls need someone to tell them who their baby's father is on TV?

Why do poor people with bad credit have to pay more to borrow money, while the rich pay less to borrow now that's not even funny?

Why is my 40-year-old cousin John still living at home with his mother? Why do people call me African when we do not call them European, Asian, or other?

Why can't I eat just anyone's pork and why are so many black people in court?

Why do homeless people seem to live in some of the coldest places? Why do good people, of all religions, walk by them without looking in their faces?

Why do people in customer service seem to be so darn mean? Why does Mr. Chris want me to call him Ms. Christine?

Why does Aunt Brenda live with Ms. Wanda who looks like a man? How is it that people have been dying forever but graveyards never run out of land?

Why do police write traffic tickets while people are getting robbed? Why do so many people want handouts without getting a job?

Why did Michael Vick get 2 years in prison for fighting dogs as a sport, while a drunk driver can kill a human and get off with probation from court?

Momma, why do some people still live on plantations? And what is a third world country-Is that how the United States looks down at other nations?

Why do I hate the police & why do I have to check behind my teachers? Why do we not trust politicians & why do we have to keep an eye on clergy & preachers?

I know you might not have all the answers, but these issues have me shaking my head. When you get the answers let me know but for now, I will just go to bed.

HIGH ROAD

Why do I always have to take the high road,
while others get away with pouring out hate
by the truck load?

I have to love my enemies and forgive them
when they attack.
I am even told to turn the other cheek after
I have been smacked.

Others get away with throwing dirt and
causing me trouble, but I have to take the moral high ground instead
of busting their bubble.

While dealing with a vindictive mother or even a deadbeat father,
I have to take a path of honor.

When can I fight back instead of always being on the defense?
When am I allowed to pick a side instead of riding on the moral
fence?

Things would not be so bad if people did not get my humbleness
confused,

because most view meekness as a sign of weakness which is far from
being true.

I will continue to take the high road so I will not

be condemned, but I hope you know that some people are alive only because it is illegal to kill them.

I will take the hard rights and avoid the easy wrongs,
I will avoid fights and attempt to always get along.

Actually, when have you ever resolved a dispute during a verbal altercation?

Generally, arguments just cause more problems and relationship frustration.

I will continue to do the right things even if it means I might get kicked around.

I will spread love and happiness as I take the high road to a higher ground.

RACISM OR SEXISM
LET'S GROW

Here is a question I want you to ponder, has America been more racist or sexist in the past? This is not a class, but your task is to just think, do not shrink to this,

Step up and drink from this educational faucet.
I can hear and feel the wheels turning, mental burning, third eyes yearning to learn.

It may be hard to recognize this, but America has clearly been more sexist. Let's go, history has shown how American feels about blacks. The systematic harassment, hounding, pounding, hatred, hunting, abuse, and loathing. So, why did white lawmakers give black men the right to vote before their wives, mothers, sisters, and daughters?

Full Stop! Now let's go as we grow with the understanding that this right was given to men so they could maintain control, we know, see, white men felt like they already had control of their wives.

Face it, America has been both racist and sexist. Hostile and oppressive and the trick is, some women act like they cannot see this while others are working hard to fix this.

If sexism was not here to stay, then why are women still fighting for equal pay? This is not something black men crave. Why, just why are men afraid, to follow a woman's leadership today, when most of us were raised by women!

WHY MIGRATE

Since the first person beat the crap out of another, there has been migrations.
Since leadership was based on strength and dominance people have relocated.

Since power and not intelligence ruled, people left Wakanda looking to form another nation.
Since the first military took over another country, there has been immigration.

Since there has been extreme cold, flooding, or famine – people have continued to migrate.

America has stood with open arms welcoming all because that is actually what made this country great.
In other countries, if you are born from a poor family, you will always be poor, you cannot rehabilitate.

But in America it is not where you start, it is how you assimilate up the food chain and your social status.

Check the records and you will see, that is why many other countries (France) hates us.

A long with our arrogance, financial dominance, freedoms, and reckless vocabulary. Do not forget our music, fashion, movies, and most important, our military. Joining the United States military has always been one of the fastest routs to citizenship along with money, marriage, or some type of committed relationship.

Today, Germany and other countries stand in the place where America once stood. American immigrants close our boarders to other immigrants, such hypocrisy will never be understood.
Once American minorities learn another language and realize how other countries look at them with awe. America will start to lose its "Vibranium" as we all start to move abroad.

A NOTE TO SUICIDE (FOR THOSE CONSIDERING SUICIDE)

Good morning suicide!
Just wanted you to know that I will not give up on my life.
I will not throw in the towel and stop my fight.
You are no longer in my line of sight.
Giving into you is just not right.
You will not get me to put out my own light.

Good afternoon suicide!
I hope you are having a very bad day.
I just stopped by to pray,
that others will not join you today,
and that you would just go away.
I am not afraid,
to look you in the face and tell you to get the hell away.

Every day you live, you set suicide back.
Every minute you breathe, you cause suicide to fail.
Every person you bless, you put suicide to shame.
So today, suicide gets no credit and we cast no blame.
We kept suicide from claiming another name.

Good night suicide, life has beaten you once again.
I am here to protect my dear friend.
We walk in victory and not in sin,

because this is only a temporary state, we are all in.
Our goal is to walk with the Mighty One in Heaven!

No additions to you suicide, you have just been told.
Not another innocent life and not another lost soul.

Another troubled family will not have to clean up suicide's mess.
One less statistic,
one less phone call,
one less coffin,
one less ride,
one less funeral,
less wet eyes.
So much less pain,
and a lot of unnecessary shame.
Less guilt and even less blame.
We even have to clean up fewer blood stains.
Good morning suicide,
today there is one less life you will gain,
yes, one less soul for you to claim!

EAT RIGHT

(A poetic salute to Mr. Peter J. D'Adamo book "Eat Right for Your Blood Type")

Did you know the foods you eat react with your blood and body chemically?
Eating food favorable to your blood type will help your body digest more efficiently.

When you are young and active, your body has a better chance to deal with the harsh things you eat. As you age, if you continue to eat those foods, then you are setting your body up for defeat.

Eating right can help you lose weight, prevent disease, and it may give you more energy.

Consuming the wrong things cause your body to work harder, fatigue faster, and feel elderly.

Food is fuel, it should give you energy, and it should make you feel your best.

There are no substitutes for human blood so here are some blood facts for you to digest.

If you have O-blood, then you are called the universal donor because you can donate red blood cells to anybody.

It is the most common and oldest blood type. If you have positive or negative blood, your diet should be high in protein, heavy on lean meats, poultry, fish, and vegetables. You can eat this because bodies with O-blood have higher levels of stomach acid for digestion.

Your diet should be light on beans, dairy, and especially grains. Grains have a way of inflaming and breaking down your auto-immunity system.

If you have A-blood then your body thrives on a meat-free diet, heavy on fruits, vegetables, beans, legumes, and whole grains. Ideally, organic, and fresh foods work best for you because you tend to have sensitive immune system.

Improving your diet can result in high performance, mental clarity, greater vitality, increased longevity, and decreased risk to cancer, diabetes, and cardiovascular disease.

If you have B-blood then you should avoid chicken, corn, wheat, buckwheat, lentils, tomatoes, peanuts, and sesame seeds. These foods fatigue your body, cause fluid retention, and cause a severe drop in blood sugar.

Your body reacts well to green vegetables, eggs, low-fat dairy, and certain meats such as goat, lamb, mutton, rabbit, and venison.

Finally, if you have the AB-blood which is very rare, then you are the universal donor of plasma. For AB people yogurt, dairy, tofu, green vegetables, and seafood such as mahi-mahi, red snapper, salmon, sardines, and tuna are good for you.

Because you tend to have low stomach acid, you should avoid caffeine, alcohol, and smoked or cured meats because they may cause stomach cancer. AB-blood is the youngest of all blood types and AB-blood people can receive blood from all other blood types.

I hope you have gained from this information. Read Dr. D'Adamo's book "Eat Right for Your Blood Type" as it gives you a full range of foods that are made for your blood type.

CHIVALRY IS ALIVE

Chivalry is not dead, but it will not live without
your assistance.

It cannot make it without your persistence.
You, me, we, have got to stop taking the path of least resistance.

Let's grow, learn, move forward see, teaching is my mission.

My goal is to change your mental condition.
Now, the first rule is to keep the female in the safest position.

Understand, at times you may follow or lead, and you should always
care.

We open doors and they sit first as we always hold chairs.
Here are some more chivalry tips of which you should be aware.

Always help her with her coat, on or off.
Lead her down the escalator and off the elevator.
Follow her up an escalator and into the elevator.

Make sure you go to the door when you want to pick her up for a date.

Her safety and comforter are what you should monitor and regulate.

Ensure she is properly strapped in when she gets into your vehicle's seat

Keep her in the safer position, away from traffic, when you walk the street.

Ask her what she would like to eat, then order her meal and make sure you cover the check.

Chivalry is basically placing women on a pedestal; it does not mean you are henpeck.

Be courteous, respectful, honest, and keep your word.
Being chivalrous is easy, just do what is right, do not be deterred.

NEW YEAR

Some New Year Resolutions you might want to consider.
From Mr. Speaker to you with love!

1. Forgive someone
2. Help someone and take nothing in return
3. Strive to better yourself in some way
4. Reduce or eliminate your debts
5. Do something you have always wanted to do
6. Make a conscious effort not to lie
7. Reach out to an old friend
8. Remember your friend's birthdays and contact them
9. Take nothing that is not yours
10. Work on smiling and greeting people with eye contact
11. Love an adult that is not a family member
12. Love more and judge less

DEATH OF A WARRIOR

Have you ever spoken to someone for what you knew would be the last time, last, I love you, last how are you feeling, and they lied?

I'm doing ok nephew, all is well, lies.
They shoot you a smile, while dealing with cancer trials.
All while dying, me, I cannot stop crying.
I would rather fight a person twice my size,
than to fight emotion flowing from my eyes.
Losing this battle after a string of victories,
while actively reaching back for life's memories.

Warriors die slowly usually alone and sad because their battle scars have driven them mad, and others away.

See those scars also remind warriors, that they lived.

They remind them of days long past and these scars make those days seem close.

Memories can open covered wounds, bring fresh tears, old fears, bad thoughts, and unfixable regrets.

Regrets for decisions made commands given.
Memories of those who died and those who were left living.
Warriors thrive while carrying other's issues,
but many times, they fail when it comes to carrying their own.

HOW TO DIE

No one really knows how much life we have to live but there is a question I want to ask.

Would you prefer to leave this life slow or fast?

Dying fast equals no planning, no reflection, less pain, no farewells, and less suffering for the individuals. But the family could have years of regret, prolong suffering, and a tremendous amount of remorse.

Dying slowly could mean more suffering, increased pain, more trips to the doctor, higher medical bills, and space. Space to say, "I am sorry, farewell, please forgive me, that is not what I meant, or I love you."

It also gives space for you to put things in a trust, write a will, get closure, or to right or see someone you miss dearly once again.

You can clear your browser history, say farewell, record some messages, have your last laugh or cry, and to see who really does care.

Death is coming no matter how healthy or how spiritual you might be.

The question still remains, what do you think is the best way to leave?

MR. & MRS. DISAGREEABLE

Hello, you may not know who you are,
so, I will describe you with a few bars.

When you listen or read, you seem to only look for points
to disagree, then you readdress.
You say no to everything even when the answer is actually yes!

You will overlook ten good statements to fight about one segment.
Then you think you are helping but even your friends are
tired of your negative comments.

You always find faults with other individuals you may not even know.
The grass in never greener with you because around you, it will not
even grow.

You seem to think fighting is helpful when the word no comes out
your mouth and from your chest.
All you do is spit negative vibes and kill any type of progress.

No one wants to share with you.
No one feels like they can grow with you.
People are always leaving you.
They will have to grow in spite of you.
You have such a negative attitude.

Some individuals make people happy wherever they go
but you Mrs. Disagreeable, you make people happy only
when you go.

Mr. Disagreeable we always know where you have been
and what you are up to, because we can see all the burnt bridges left
behind you.

I know you do not agree with what I am telling you.
Saying no, well that is just what you do.

We are moving forward, and we want you to come to.
It is not hard to be positive, just slightly alter your view.
First, you are going to have to drop that negative attitude.

Then you need to increase your level of love and not be so rude. I am
just dropping some lines with the hope that
something will get through.

Maybe you do not know anyone I am describing in this composition.
Then I suggest you take a look in the mirror because
you could be the one who fits this description.

JUST DO NOT LIKE

When people walk against the flow, I dislike this.
When individuals drive slow in the fast lane,
I dislike this too.

When someone lies and especially those that will not even try, I do
not like their lack of effort.

When poets explain their poems, disrespectful.

When someone refuses to wash their hands or
their ass, offensive.

Especially when someone will not let me be great, that is clearly
someone trying to generate hate.

Here is one, when someone rudely interrupts others conversation or
when someone disrespects their parents and then look for a blessing.

Hypocrisy, thieves, cheaters, anchovies, and hummus
Especially bullies who take advantage of us.

Bad grammar, bad breath, and boys masquerading as men.

People who cough or sneeze and refuse to cover their face.

Weak leaders, waiting in long lines, and individuals who throw rocks
and hide their hands.

I hate missing a good poem and I especially hate the end of an open mic.

I'm Sick of

1. Bosses that appreciate you after you are gone.
2. People who stand in other's walking path.
3. Snow in April.
4. People who have the correct answer and will not tell you!
5. People screaming my name out in public.
6. Funky people in really tight spaces.
7. Dropping something important down the side of the driver's seat of my car.
8. Being late for something and having car trouble.
9. People who owe you money and act like they do not remember.
10. People who repeat themselves over and over.
11. All the Captain Obvious out there.
12. Food that looks good but taste horrible
13. Food that is good for you and taste horrible.
14. Food you like but it is not good for you.
15. People trying to sing but they cannot.
16. Friends who do not tell friends things they need to know.
17. People who do not know where something is but still try to give directions, WHY?
18. People begging for money.
19. People who disrespect their parents or the elderly!
20. HYPOCRITES

THE MOB

The mob rules everything around us,
right or wrong, this is preposterous.

Maybe this is a repeat of things from the past.
Fact is that democracy may not last.

Who can say "the majority knows what is best?"
They have been wrong before, I must confess.

We have laws in place to protect this democracy.
The mob should never override civil authority.

Cell phones and social media give many people
their reports.
Propelled by the media, you are guilty before
you get to court.

The mob and our laws do not always agree.
Just look at the verdicts we have had in history.

Think and decide for yourself what is right or wrong.
We choose individually if we are going to get along.

The mob rules everything around us
right or wrong, this is preposterous.

Follow your heart and in God keep your trust.

SHOT

The first time you get shot,
shock crashes,
immortality passes, and your
life flashes.

Pain stuns, blood runs, and you pray not to hear
another gun, shot.
Repeat, reload, better aim, bang.

In a Quaker Oat's instant, you thank and question God.
See, He saved you from that barrage, but why?
Is this a Job like test?
While life is leaking out my chest or
is my earthly run done.

No more grace for me to remain in this place.
My judgement has begun.
From this, I cannot run.
Who gave this little and weak person a gun?

As blood drains, pain remains,
to remind me that I still have life.
Do not put me on ice. I think I am alright.
In me, there is still some fight and
I am not walking towards any lights.

I can breathe, feel, hear, and see.
WOW, God has blessed me.

Oh damn, Bang!

FATHER WOUNDS

Shots fired, direct hits, but a gun was not used.
A father wounds in many ways, please do not be confused.

The father is a critical part of the family construct, and his poor actions can damage the family and mess individuals all up.

A father wounds through: Alcoholism, drugs, abuse, lies, not paying child support, and showing a lack of compassion. He wounds by not being there, giving poor advice, not keeping his word, outside children, and by having no direction.

Men battle many obstacles like unemployment, health, and depression is one of the worse.
I understand that some of his issues really are a form of a generational curse.

A father should know that his family needs him, even if only for protection.
They also need his encouragement, guidance, direction, advice, compassion, and correction.

Far too many things divide or separate fathers
from their obligations.

Crime, prison, drugs, strip clubs, and sidepieces break down the family formation.

A father's wounds impact both sons and daughters separate or together. Sons may recover faster while these wounds tend to haunt daughters forever.

Some impacts of a father's wounds are; I cannot keep or maintain a relationship, I cannot ride a bike, I cannot swim, I keep attracting the wrong person, I cannot listen to authority, I lack discipline, I cannot keep a job, I am a womanizer, or I exploit men exotically.

Remarkably, wounds heal, and they heal faster when they are treated. Here is one solution so your father's wounds won't be repeated.

On a piece of paper, write all the words that describe your father or his actions, understand.
Then speak those words out-loud one last time, fold the paper, and throw it into the trash can.
Pray to our Heavenly Father for the strength to forgive.
Ask God to help you get past your father's wounds so your full life, you can live.

Please do not stand in judgement of your father as that could make things worse. God gifted your father with you because God knew you had the strength to forgive and break this curse.

Father's wounds are a serious matter that must be addressed.
Use God's love and your forgiveness as ingredients to your success.

FATHERS AND DAUGHTERS

Daughters tend to marry men who are just like their fathers.

Let me tell you a story about a young lady who should not have bothered.

Her father was not much of a rolling stone,
but he did bring most of his daily issues and problems home.

He then laid them at the feet of his loving wife,
through arguments, both day and night.
Verbal, mental, physical, and even fist fights.

He had to be right, even when he was wrong,
same sound, same lyrics, same old tired song.

This generational issue skipped a verse and then got worse.
He had no idea his baby girl was the next victim
of this curse.

No, he never put his hands on her physically,
She just married a man that was suffering like her father mentally.

He was young, handsome, ambitious, you know the type.
Hard working, misunderstood guy who gets beat up by life.

Justice is something he never receives.

He deals with obstacles like you would not believe,
and faces frustrations you cannot conceive,
mainly because his skin is the color of ebony.

He feels beat down by ivory.
So, he then beats the mother of his seed.

Daily, physically, violence fueled by Hennessey,
but not for the children to see.

Well, the father, thought this was kept out of sight, but domestics
scars do not always heal overnight.
They are passed on to the next generation as they become visible in
the light.

Father, which way is right?
Up seems to go left and like a bald Sampson, without you, I have no
might.
The father prayed, please extract this cancer from my family and life.

Now as I lay here prostrate,
I pray to you Lord this curse to break.

If my daughter wakes up with you this eve,
I pray for forgiveness, her soul, and those that grieve.

I come to you Father with an open heart and open hands,
because you alone God have the power to heal the land!

KAPPA ALPHA PSI CENTENNIAL (114) SLAM

We have been around a long time and yes, we have done some things wrong
But we've made corrections and our founder's dream is alive and going strong

We were not the 1st, and we were not the last but, we are the only fraternity with a touch of class.
We have survived world wars and the big depression, and we will survive all of life's many lessons.

Because Kappa's are here to stay get that through your head. And ladies what you heard is true, we are definitely good in bed.

See a true Kappa man knows how to make you feel good all the time. And more importantly we know loving you starts by making love to your mind.

Ladies, chivalry is not dead, being a gentleman, is not a thing of the past. We are wearing crimson and cream, and we are up to any task.

Some people go hard in the paint but for Kappa's that is not quite the right image.
See, this is a man's game so that is why we control that line of scrimmage.

Scoring touchdowns, hitting home runs we are always putting that work in!

Just watch those Nupes and you will see that all we do is WIN . . .
WIN . . . WIN!

We are wanted locally, nationally, and even worldwide,
and we are the only men who know the true meaning of Phi Nu Pi

Been called Casanova, Pretty Ricky, Prince Charming, and even Don
Won as names and just for the record, Nupes invented stepping with
the canes.

A play fact is, we also invented pimping check the records and watch
how we flow.
Nupes were even the first to be called "Captain Save a Ho."

College educated well paid and talented in bed.
Do not get upset with me as I am just repeating what your lady said.

To be a Nupe you must have more bounce to the ounce even while
posing,
because like the good book says, many are called but only a few are
chosen.

Nupes come in all shapes sizes and colors, but achievement is what
actually bonds us as brothers.

Look who is leading the pack and winning the race. Other fraternities
just cannot keep up with
our frantic pace.

We are gentlemen not dogs, nerds, or copycats either: Nupes are the
originals as we are on top while the rest are just bottom feeders.

So, to our founders who had this unique dream that was so vivid and
clever.

114 years later, those well-dressed, pretty boys are still all about
achievement in every field of human endeavor.

GREEK SLAM

I could never be an Alpha so let me tell you why,
First, they do not know the meaning of Phi Nu Pi

Alpha Phi Alpha, I must give you your props as you were the first,
But when it comes to brother hood you are the worst.

You do not even have to pledge Alpha from what I remember. They
will just let you in and call you an "Honorary Member."

I looked at organizations, I have checked out the majority,
and hands down, the Alphas act more like a sorority.

There is just no way I could be an Omega you see.
Because I was a man far before I joined a fraternity.

That's not the only reason I could not go there way,
I do not have rabies and I take a shower every day.

Omegas and Kappas have been close if you study the past,
The big difference is in public Omegas sometimes show no class.

The bottom line, I was already a man, not a dog so here me please,
go to the vet and get a shot for those flees!

Mr. Sigma, are you laughing at the other Greeks I am talking about?
That is funny because it is your organization the Kappas, Ques, and
Alphas joke about at their frat house.

Your founders had no vision, few original thoughts, and no direction for your concept.
So, they stole most of their ideas from the Alphas, Kappas, and Omegas, quiet as it is kept.

When you step, you look like a mixture of Kappas, Ques, and Delta Sigma Theta.
And actually, your organization's name should be Phi Beta Imitator.

Look at your hand sign if you think what I am saying is not true.
You flash the Six and the Yo, like the Alpha and Kappas as you throw your hands to intimate the Ques.

And if you check like I hope you would,
you will see the Sigmas simply have no concept of brother hood.

Now let me be thorough, let me address them all.
You are not a fraternity if you meet in a mason hall.

Look up in the air and what do you see OH my.
Check out those brothers of Kappa Alpha Psi.

We were not the first and we were not the last,
but we are the only frat with a touch of class.

We have brothers from north to south and east to west
And the ladies will tell you that we make love the best.

I am a brother of Kappa Alpha Psi.
We are those pretty boys and that is no lie.

Don't mean to brag and I don't mean to boast,
but the ladies love those Kappa men the most.

Achievement is what we are about which is not that clever,
but you must achieve in every field of human endeavor.

So, you can talk about me all that you can,
but you know none of you are worthy of being a Kappa Man!

So, why you are standing there with your face cracked and looking frozen.

Remember, with the NUPES, many are called but only a few are chosen.

ART (THE FORWARD TO AMERICAN GRAVEYARD) WRITTEN BY MR. SPEAKER WITH CREDIT TO FRED R. BARNARD.

It has been said that a picture is worth one thousand words, but I say a poem paints one thousand pictures. Picturing things with your mind is poetic. Observing with your eyes is artistic, while seeing things with your heart, now that is beautiful. Art in all forms transcends and breaks through language barriers. Art travels, translates, and communicates to individuals who cannot hear.

In American Graveyard, you will take an artistic journey to places only the mind and heart are allowed to visit. These 14 different contributors have created a collage of artistry that will amaze you from start to finish. Beauty is in the eyes of the beholder, so let the pages of this book reveal the beauty within you.

It is difficult for good and bad to co-exist. Generally, love and hate are present in all circumstances, and at the end of the day, we choose which one dominates. As love, understanding, and compassion increase, gun violence and hate have to decrease.

This book is a call to make love not war, put down your guns, and write, paint, create, to unite. Your charge is to be inspired by the talent and love on display in these pages. Allow American Graveyard to challenge you to grow and be filled with all things beautiful. Then together, we can reduce gun violence by judging less and loving more.

I SCARE WHITE PEOPLE

I scare white people when I am happy, and I scare them when I talk.
I scare white people when I'm upset, and I even scare them when I walk.

I scare them if and when I speak.
I scare them in dark alleys or on lit streets.

I scare white people if I am educated.
I really scare them when I am uneducated.

We scare white people when two or more of us have private conversations.
We really scare them when we out maneuver or think them during any type of negotiations.

We scare them on elevators and in all parking lots.
I'm in a seven series, you are driving an old dodge hornet, and you think I want what you've got?
Fear even keeps white women from even looking my direction while at a traffic stop.

We scare white people if we live next to them or far away.
We also scare white people during sporting events we all play.

Look, I scare white people when I do not even try.
We scare white people on days that end in "Y."

Truth be told, we scare Asians, Hispanics, and
other Black people too,
because you all believe everything the media tells you.

The facts are, there are more white people in jail, and they commit
more crimes every single day.

You are afraid of me when you should be looking out for white
criminals in biker gangs, movie shooters like James Holmes and
bombers like Timothy McVeigh.

I scare white people because they just do not
understand me.
They actually hate and berate me.

They mistreat me, give max sentences to me and they are prejudice
towards me.
White people do everything but love me.

Well, except white women because once they get to know me, they
cannot get enough of me.
They fight for my seed until the day comes when they scream rape
and point at me.

While in jail, they still visit me, but all this makes white men and
black women angry with me.

I have tried to blend in by speaking proper English, wearing suits,
and getting a degree or two.
At the end of the day, I still scare the shit out of white people no
matter what I do.

WHAT LAST

One day you will realize that your Soul is the only thing about you that is immortal.

No matter how much you feed the flesh, it keeps
getting hungry.

No matter how many weights you lift you will still lose strength.
No matter how far your run or how much you exercise, your flesh will grow tired.

You may have heard it said that only what we do
for God will last.

But many feed, build, and promote that flesh but it is still dying while our immortal souls go neglected.

Rules to live by:

If it brings you closer to God, then it is of God, but if it takes you away from God, leave it alone.

Avoid users, complainers, blamers, competitors, and abusers.

According to Mr. Richard Bach, "If you love someone, set them free. If they come back, they're yours; if they do not, they never were.

Today, from me, this advice would never be given.

If you love someone then you better hold on tight or you could be alone the rest of your life.

If you love someone, then be prepared to fight.
Because life will attack that love on sight.

If you love someone then you need to know it takes work.
It also takes prayer, church, and a strong supportive network.

So, if you love someone hold on tight for as long as you can, before the world, illness, or deaths snatches them from your hands.

EVERYONE SHOULD

Everyone should:

complete high school no matter what,
serve two years in the military or some organization,
attend college or a trade school,
and learn one foreign language.

Everyone should walk or run a mile,
Learn to ride a bike,
drive a car,
and learn to swim.

Everyone should love someone outside your family,
travel to at least two other countries.
fly in a plane,
and do some community service.

Everyone should read a book,
watch a movie,
see a play,
and write their own story.

Everyone should write a poem,
hear and tell a joke,
live alone at least once,
belong to a team,
love, laugh, and cry.

Everyone should live!

CAPTAIN OBVIOUS

Many of you may know people who feel the need to tell you some of the most ridiculous things.

Sometimes it is because they are trying to be helpful while other times, I have the foggiest.
That is why I have labeled these individuals with the term, "Captain Obvious."

Allow me to explain so we can discuss. We both witness something that happens right in front of us.

Maybe it is just something simple or some common thing you would see any day. Captain Obvious still feels compelled to tell you about it any way.
Nice individuals just listen and smile while Captain Obvious gets their point across.

They are thinking about how much time they just lost.
You think they want to listen to you tell them this old news. They are really hoping you do not decide to conduct a review.

At that point, it could be time to give you a clue that you do not have to tell obvious news, giving others the blues, and making them want to be rude.

Captain Obvious I know you are out there. I am not trying to hurt your feelings or act like I do not care.

I'm just asking that you think before you open your mouth and realize who you are talking to and what you are talking about.

If you realize you are speaking to someone who knows more about the subject than you, then please get a clue, save the world from your unnecessary conversation, and find something else to do.

In order to keep you from feeling singled out or picked on, I am addressing this whole audience. Please do not get mad and start a fuss, just because I have called you

Captain Obvious.

SLIPPERY FOUNDATION

Where do you go when your foundation is gone?

What do you do when you lose your mom?

What do you hold on to during an earthquake?
Can a doctor actually heal heartbreak?

You fall with no end or stop.
All you do is hit tree limbs or steps as you drop.

Maybe you do not want to hit escape to end,
because then you would have to face your sins.

Where does a King go for peace?
Is there a safe place for his tears to be released?

What do you do because it really hurts,
when you lose the first guide you had on earth?

What happens when you lose your very first friend?
Is it even possible for your heart to ever mend?

I have lost before but never like this!
I would do just about anything for another
hug and a kiss.

HOW TO LEAD

Are you a leader or a follower?

The correct answer is I am both.

Truth is no one wants to follow a bad leader

The first thing to leadership is followership.

Only a small percentage of us are leaders but
all of us are followers.

So why is followership never taught especially when poor followers
can destroy any plan?
Leadership classes are almost everywhere.

Maybe it is the word followership which is interchangeable with
helper, supporter, strengthener,
or aide.

In the Bible, the Savior demonstrates servant leadership while God
plays the role of Helper.

God aids, helps, strengthens, and aids His people.
So, what makes us too good to follow?

Good help is reliable, trustworthy, loyal, dependable, and
knowledgeable and good help prays.

Good help fills gaps, rebounds, blocks, and tackles so the team wins.

Unsung heroes which everyone knows, they are the glue and the heart.
Every great leader is an exceptional follower.
Anyone that can't follow is not worthy to be followed.

Have you prayed for your leaders lately or do you speak negatively about them while putting hate into the air?

Be an effective follower, support system and friend. Follow God's example and stay true so that the team wins. No one wants to follow a bad leader. Be the follower you would want to have.

ADVICE – LEADER TO LEADER!

(Me to Me - Write a poem to yourself)

We have come a long way baby, and this story is not over yet. You are carrying a lot of weight on those shoulders, do not forget.

To whom much is given, much is required. Recite that verse the next time you get tired. Slow down and enjoy these moments, this journey, and these trials.

You have the heart of a teacher, spirit of giving, and a passion to help others. If you lose your way, think about the legacy of your mother, your father, grandparents and so many others who prayed for you.

Even at a slower pace, you must stay focused and on target. Remember, life is a circle you need to know this is true. You will reap what you sew, so what you plant comes back to you.

You still have to do twice as much just to stay even, that has not changed so keep achieving. Execute your vision board and stop always looking for perfection. Let the hurtful things said not be a distraction.

Learn and grow as every mistake does not require an instant correction. Even rejections are still connections and miss-steps are lessons. Stay on mission and do not waste time responding to deflections.

Just because someone knows better does not always mean they will do better!

You are a King's legacy, a slave's dream, a father's hope, and a mother's glory.

Run with purpose, plan continually, always be ready to execute, and keep writing this story.

Lead yourself with your head but lead others
with your heart.

Stay ready for success and remain mindful that the enemy wants to take you apart.

Power, greed, envy, and even success have been the downfall of individuals much greater than you.

Follow your vision, your passion, run towards your purpose, and see things through.

Rest with a pen and pad and teach with an eye on other people's capabilities.

Seek ways to give back, remain productive, and hold to God's boundless possibilities.

Show compassion when you should not and spread smiles during difficult times.

Pause to rejuvenate, meditate, and we should all remember to congratulate those under your noses.

This is what your grandmother meant when she told you to "Take time to smell the roses!"

You are the result of prayers, you are a leader, you are freedom, and you are an inspiration.

You are a champion, an overcomer, a victor, a survivor, a hero, and a legend to your congregation.

One last very important nugget I need to deliver completely.

You must remain accountable because power corrupts, and absolute power still corrupts absolutely.

See Mr. Speaker, you are the dream realized of James and Catherine Sears, Hershel and Rosetta Sears, and Ida and Charles Mitchell. Keep achieving!

R. I. P. REST IN POETRY

In Memory of Dr. Hollis H. Pruitt

Rest in poetry my dear friend.
May words travel with you as you ascend.

You have blessed so many with your poetic blends.
Now you lie silent as your earthly journey has
come to an end.

May you find heavenly peace free of any earthly pains.
I pray the angels see you and know you by your name.

May you find answers to questions and solutions to
life's mysteries.

May your ancestors find you and may you find the truth about black
history.

It was a treat to be mentored by you.
It was a blessing to share words as poetically I grew.

I pray you lived a life without any regrets.
It is your love affair with words that I will never forget.

You, the poetic icon, a prolific writer, and poet maker,
you manipulated words and you were a stereotype breaker.

I cherish the little time we shared here on earth at poetic venues.]

I am thankful that I came to Barns & Noble for poetry and do not worry, it will continue.

Your legacy is secure, and your legendary status confirmed.

Write in peace Dr. Pruitt as truly your victory and rest has been earned.

Thank you for everything,
and thank God for sending you to be such a blessing!

THE CLOSER (READ AT THE END OF AN OPEN MIC EVENT)

Conclusion

WOW, I had a great time and I hope you did too,
but right now, I must let you know that poetry for tonight is through.

I want to thank each and every poet for helping with this cause.
So please join me as we give them one final applause.

Please feel free to let the poets know how you feel about what they said tonight.
It's your opportunity to inspire them so they will continue to write.

I hope these artists have inspired you to come back again
Maybe they have encouraged you to bring out some of your friends.

You do not have to leave continue to relax and enjoy this place.
DJ Panama will keep the music flowing, so everyone can feel this base.

If you have enjoyed yourselves then let me know.
Make sure you tell the owner before you go home.

If you were inspired by something you heard
Then come back and see us on January 23rd.

Yes, we will return for more spoken word.

So, get your poems ready so you can be heard.

Just write down your thoughts and let your words
come out.

Then at the next poetry night you can let us know what you are all
about.

See Mr. Speaker if you have questions about upcoming events.

Make sure we have your social media information because that is
how this information is sent.

February will be Valentines so come out prepared to play your part.

We have something really special planned because we want to warm
your HEARTS!

So, thanks for coming out we hope to see you again.
Poetry is done for tonight, down goes the MIC so you can pick up
your PEN.

www.ingramcontent.com/pod-product-compliance
Lightning Source LLC
Chambersburg PA
CBHW021622120626
46545CB00001B/361